Dancing BEARS

by Paul Ward

This edition first published in paperback by
Michael Terence Publishing in 2024
www.mtp.agency

Copyright © 2024 Paul Ward

Paul Ward has asserted the right to be identified as
the author of this work in accordance with the
Copyright, Designs and Patents Act 1988

ISBN 9781800947863

No part of this publication may be reproduced, stored
in a retrieval system, or transmitted, in any form or
by any means, electronic, mechanical, photocopying,
recording or otherwise, without the prior
permission of the publisher

Cover images
Copyright © www.123rf.com

Cover design
Copyright © 2024 Michael Terence Publishing

Part One

1

Have you ever wondered about life and what you can expect from it? Have you ever asked yourself questions about love, and where love fits in and why we have it? If you have lost love, or the love of your life. We are an intelligent species, or so we say, and yet these life questions, which are very important, are very hard to answer. We can look at other species, and by studying them we can answer questions about that species, and yet with the human race, there seems to be anomalies and complexities far too great to enable us to do this valuable thing.

This book attempts to unravel the mysteries of the human race, to answer all manner of questions about our makeup, about how we came to be here and what rules of nature apply to us.

Is there any reason to undertake writing such a book? What is the purpose of it? There is a saying: if it's not broken don't fix it. But when looking at the world today, and the history of the world as we know it, there is reason to do something about it. There have been too many wars, there is too much violence, the divorce rate is too high, there is theft, racial abuse, antisocial behaviour, and the list goes on.

We think of problems on a personal level, on a social level, and even on a world level. Whichever level you are looking at, there is work to be done. My chosen route to finding the knowledge I sought was to go back to the beginning, back to the point in time when we started to evolve as human beings. The task which I set myself was so vast that it would take me over a year of deep thinking to complete, and I then found it to be the start of a whole new line of philosophy.

It was not my intention to write a book, that was not what made me start thinking. It was my experiences of life which made me want to find answers. Having found out what I found out, I thought it impossible to keep to myself. I felt a real need to share my thoughts.

When I first wrote *Dancing Bears*, and this is the third time of writing it, I did not believe in God. It was important that at that time this be the case, because I would identify the need to have a set of rules to live our lives by in order to get the very best we can as individuals and as a society. I was amazed to find out about the existence of the Ten Commandments, a set of rules just like I was thinking about. I could not possibly imagine how such a set of rules could exist without having gone through the same lines of philosophy that I went through with *Dancing Bears*.

If you think of *Dancing Bears* as a giant jigsaw puzzle, we have hundreds of pieces of the puzzle, but no picture on the lid of the box to copy. We also have more pieces than we need in order to complete the puzzle. If you like, we have two hundred pieces of jigsaw for a one-hundred-piece puzzle. So where do the extra hundred pieces come from, the confusing pieces? These pieces come from different places. They come from expectation, i.e., you expect or want the picture to look different than it actually does, and so you invent some pieces. We also have accepted new changes in the way that we behave, with the mistaken view that this modern ideology is correct, so these new pieces should not exist. If you think about human behaviour as pieces of the puzzle, then all the pieces must fit together; there must be no extra pieces left over, and no pieces missing.

If you are going on a journey and you don't have a map but know roughly where you are meant to be going, you sometimes take a wrong turn at a junction. If you get lost but end up at the same junction again, you will know not to make the same mistake again, and so you will have a better idea of how to get to your destination. If our destination is to achieve the very best we can from life, for ourselves, for our loved ones, for our society, for our country, and for our world, then would it not be fantastic if we had a map or blueprint to follow? Because when we take the wrong turn, people get hurt, and it is not always easy to get back on the right route. Also, sometimes when we are on a journey, we pass a side road and we like the look of it and go down it. It may turn out that it is a dead end with a rubbish tip at the end of it. No real harm is done, you just don't go down that road again. However, when human beings go down a dead end because they liked the look of it, it can end up a real mess.

You see, if we did have that map, we would know our route, and we would not make mistakes and we would know what was down the side roads. All in all, we need this map. As a species, we are all of us, as individuals, capable of extremely good or bad behaviour. Sometimes we live side by side with our neighbours for centuries in perfect harmony, and then we end up fighting or killing our neighbours. Why? Sometimes we fall in love and live happily ever after, and sometimes we fall in love and end up hating our partners. Why? If we had this blueprint or map, and hence had a complete picture of what we are and require as a species, then it would be folly to disregard it.

If you accept my work as the blueprint of the human race, then you may start looking at your own life, the lives of others, maybe politicians, whole countries, the people that you love, or any person in the world.

The main point is that the laws of nature apply to every human being on the planet, and so you can analyse everyone on an equal footing. I want people everywhere to start to analyse their own lives, to look at the way they were brought up, their relationship with their loved ones, and look at their failures and successes. If you think of the influences that there are in your life, you may find that you did things wrong in your life because of various reasons. I want people to learn to forgive themselves, because I am sure that there were many reasons why they did things wrong in the past. Of course, if you feel that, on a personal level, the influences or reasons why you went wrong are there, then learn to forgive yourself. Influences on your life are real, they are genuine, they really do affect your life. Of course, if you do find that you are forgiving yourself, even if it is by degrees, then surely you should learn to forgive others. You can make allowances for other people's errors the same as you can for yourself. The influences that there are for a person are the same for everyone. It may well be that you decide to extend your ideas of forgiveness and go beyond that of an individual and look at your society and even your country. It may be that your own country has done things wrong in the past. How good it would be to be forgiven by other countries that your country has wronged, and how good it would be to forgive other countries that have wronged your own.

When I started philosophising about life, I started in the garden. I used to sit alone in my garden late at night, or early in the morning. I used to look at the stars and the plants and creatures in my garden and think to myself that the world is a very beautiful place. The natural world is that excellent thing which we admire because of its diversity and beauty. We admire it, and we are part of it. We can be the best or the worst creature the planet has ever known. We have to know as much as we can about ourselves in order to get as close to the good side as we can.

If we look at history and our own lives, we can see when good has been achieved. Where we see this, we can repeat it, and when we see the opposite we can avoid repeating it. Knowledge is not to be feared, ignorance is.

2

In looking at the birth of a new species, one would have to go back to the beginning of the evolution of that species, the very first change that triggered a chain of events which lead a new species evolving.

My interest is in the evolution of the human race. What was the single thing that came along that allowed the human race to evolve? One would have to look at the variables that there are; what things can change? First is the most obvious thing, a physical change, something that you can see. Then there is a biochemical change, a change in a creature's chemistry. There is also a change in instinct or inbuilt behaviour. There is one other variable, and that is intelligence, the degree of intelligence a creature has. One would think that the more intelligent a creature, the better its chances of survival. This is not the case, and I need to look at this in greater detail, but it is a variable.

When you look at the natural world, the degree of variation that there is of all the different creatures is astonishing. All creatures have a specific shape and size, they all have specific things to do in their lives, and they all know how to do it without thinking. Inbuilt behaviour or instinct is absolutely critical to every creature on the planet.

You could look at other creatures like birds. They are easy to observe, and there is a good variety of them. Some birds migrate every year; they know exactly where and when to go. They have never been shown a journey, but they instinctively know what to do. Also, birds know how to build a nest, they know how to mate, they know how to raise their young, they know what to eat and how to get it. There is a wide variety of insects, who all have specific jobs to do. Some spiders build webs and learn how to trap prey. They are not shown what to do, they just know it. Some insects live in colonies and have different jobs within the colony, but they all have instincts to tell them what to do and what their specific tasks are. A dog knows how to bury a bone, a cat knows how to hunt, a beaver knows how to build a lodge, a bear knows how to hibernate. It does not matter which creature you choose to look at, you will find inbuilt behaviour in every creature.

Intelligence is something which needs to be dealt with as a subject in its own right, separate from instincts, even though it effects behaviour. When looking at evolution and the behaviour of different creatures, there is a rule of nature regarding intelligence. I have thought long and hard on this subject, and I have to conclude that it is a disadvantage to be any more intelligent than you need to be, in order to survive as your species requires and necessary behaviour dictates.

Let's assume that intelligence comes along as a genetic mutation; under normal circumstances, the creature that this happens to would die. With the human race, however, this proved not to be the case. Something happened to us to change the rules of nature. What happened to us was that every time increased intelligence came along, it became an advantage to us and so became part of our makeup. The same mutations could occur for all creatures on the planet. The rate at which we progressed could have been the rate for all creatures, but it was not and it will not be.

You have to try and imagine what various creatures would be like if they became more intelligent. To explain the point we will look at a shoal of mackerel. Assume that one fish has been born with increased intelligence. This fish has observed that sharks are picking off mackerel on the edge of the shoal and decides that it would be a good idea to stay in the middle of the shoal. However, the fish on the edge of the shoal are getting all of the sand eels, and no sand eels are getting through to the middle of the shoal. The intelligent fish was not doing exactly what a good mackerel should do, that is, see sand eel, open mouth, and eat it before one of its competitors eats it, so there is no time to spend thinking. Thinking affects behaviour and there is no room for it in normal nature. The intelligent mackerel died. Whatever species you look at, you can try and imagine what would happen if intelligence crept in. In all cases except the human race, the change in behaviour would be at the detriment of the species.

I spent considerable time looking at how a new species could evolve, and what rules of nature would be applied to such an event. If we look at the variables, we have physical change, instinct change, and biochemical change. Any of these things could throw up a mutation. However, for the first change, the change that allows for a string of changes or birth of a new species, the change must not be to the detriment of the species. A small change to any of the variables could result in this, but the change must fit in with the normal way of life and not be detrimental to the species. To explain the point, I am going to the development of a new species of frog as an example. There is a species of frog, it is green and lives near water. It lies still during daylight hours, and comes out at night and eats flies. It relies on its camouflage to protect it during the daytime and, although they are good to eat, enough of them survive to sustain their species. Now, imagine one frog has been born with a genetic mutation, which induces a biochemical change to the pigment in its skin. It has become toxic and also tastes bad. Outwardly, the frog is the same as before: it is the same colour, it still comes out at night and eats flies, in fact it does exactly the same as it would normally do. However, now other changes can happen. The frog is no longer good to eat, and so a change in behaviour can happen. It can come out during the daytime when there is more to eat. The species could now physically change, its eyes would change to adapt to seeing better in daylight, and so now you see that a biochemical change allowed for a behavioural change and a physical change.

I hope that this way of explaining things works. The initial change could be in any of the variables, but the main thing is that the change must not be to the detriment of the species in its original state.

I should like to elaborate a little more on the subject of instincts. So important are they that they need looking at very closely. An instinct is inbuilt behaviour and when you do what your instinct is telling you to do, you will be rewarded. This manifests itself by way of feeling really good. When you do what your instincts are telling you to do, you feel brilliant. However, instincts are so important that not only are you rewarded for going along with it, but there is also a negative feeling or response should you not be doing what your instincts are telling you to do. I liken this to eating; not only is it pleasurable to eat but there is also a negative feeling when you do not eat, i.e., feeling hungry. You can see from this example how utterly important instincts are, that we have a reward and punishment system in operation. If you are not doing what your instincts are telling you to do, you get a bad feeling, which I call "instinct deprivation syndrome" (IDS). To explain the point, we have names for two common forms of IDS, one is "lonely". We are a group creature, and not only is it nice to have company, but the negative response is that you feel lonely. The other one is "homesick". One of our instincts is to occupy a territory and be familiar with it, you could say a place we call home. Human beings are complex creatures and have several instincts, each one being capable of rewarding or punishing according to whether or not you follow your instincts. We have such complicated lives these days and have lost track of our basic instincts, I suggest that we suffer, by a greater or lesser degree, from different IDS. What we need to do is strip the human race back to its foundations and look at what we should be doing. A lot of people suffer from depression or just feel unhappy without knowing why. They could be suffering from one or more forms of IDS. My work gives psychologists whole new lines of philosophy. It is very simple to understand and easy to apply.

I have obviously spent a great deal of time on the subject of how we came to be here, and the rules of nature that apply to us. I have run scenario after scenario through my mind, countless times I have applied logic and thought, and countless times I have rejected scenarios. However, when I had established the rules of nature and found the exact correct scenario, everything fitted in place. It made perfect sense of the human makeup, and you could apply the philosophy to any society in the world. I could apply it to myself; I am a human being with feelings and instincts of my own.

The next chapter details what we were like as a creature before the initial trigger or change that allowed us to develop into human beings. I have not gone down the road of detailing scenarios that were rejected, I just have run through the exact one as it is.

3

When looking at where we came from, we start with the obvious observation, and that is that we descended from apes. We know this because of the similarity of our appearances and because we have found bones showing the changes that have occurred to us at various stages of evolution of our species. Today, we can study apes, some are group creatures and some live solitary lives. Both of these types look similar to each other but have different behaviour.

We were group creatures, not solitary. I can say this with all certainty because it fits in with my development scenario and helps explain how we are today. We were a group creature that occupied a territory. It is important to have a territory that you are familiar with because you will know where to find food and water. The group is led by an alpha male, and so it is the instinct of both the males and females to follow a male leader. It is the instinct of the male leader that his troop or group has its basic requirements in terms of food and water; in other words, his instinct is to provide. All males want to be the leader, they are all born wanting to be the leader, and it is an instinct within all males. The instinct is driven in part by the instinct to reproduce. It is the female's instinct to want to mate with the leader, or alpha male, and it is the female's instinct to want to have young and look after and nurse the young. All males must be prepared to fight for the position of leader, for it will not be given up lightly, and the leader must be prepared to fight to hold his position. The reward is that you get to reproduce with as many females as possible and pass on your genetic information. It is important that it be like this because it ensures that a leader is not around long enough to start to reproduce with his own offspring, which is genetically a bad thing to happen. Furthermore, it is always the fittest and strongest male that leads and reproduces, and this ensures that no juvenile becomes leader because they would not be strong enough to challenge for leadership, and they would not be wise enough to lead anyway. There is another instinct which applies to the males, and this relates to conflict with other groups. It may be that the group is required to go into another group's territory. Should the group's area run out of food or water, for the survival of the group, it would be essential to extend the territory into a neighbouring territory. It is important that the group act as one, in conflict with another group. If a single individual went in on his own, he would be killed. It must be that the group engages in conflict as a unit, all males moving at the same time. If this seems like an unrealistic instinct, then you must imagine a conflict scenario. You could be taking over a neighbouring territory through absolute necessity, the lives of the whole group are at stake. The same instinct applies in the defence of your own territory. If another group is trying to take over your area, you must act together as a unit in exactly the same way. This is a brief outline of how we were before the change that allowed for our evolution to start. It is quite simple and shows what our instincts were prior to the trigger. We need to look into what would happen in this scenario if increased intelligence occurred. Imagine what would happen if we became intelligent enough to use an object as a weapon. Something as simple as picking up a rock and hitting another group member over the head with it. Imagine a young juvenile could now challenge for the role of group leader because he could now kill. Remember that all males want to become leader, and this is driven by the desire or instinct to reproduce. You would not have a young inexperienced leader of the group, because he quite simply would not know what to do. The new leader could also be killed, and then that leader could be killed, all in all we would be looking at a group with no direction or leadership and a level of violence within the group which would be totally destructive. Remember the rule: it is a disadvantage to be any more intelligent than you need to be in to be in order to survive as you are. It is the instinct of both males and females to be part of a group, to be group members, which includes forging special bonds or friendships with other group members. With regard to our instincts, you have to observe that male and female instincts are different, but both work together in a group environment. We are now in a position to list all of the instincts for the males and females of our species as we were prior to the change which triggered the beginning of our evolution. The female instincts are as follows:

1. To know or occupy a known area or territory.
2. To be a group member or be part of a group.

3. To forge special bonds or friendships with other group members.
4. To want to mate with the group leader.
5. To want young and to feed and look after them while they are young.
6. To want to stand out above other females when ready to mate.
7. To follow the leader of the group around the group's territory.
8. The instincts for the males are as follows:
9. To be familiar with a known area or territory.
10. To be part of a group.
11. To forge special bonds or friendships with other group members.
12. To want to mate with females when the females make themselves available.
13. To want to be the group leader or alpha male.
14. To challenge or fight for the position of alpha male.
15. In times of group conflict, to act as a fighting unit with the other males of the group.
16. To follow the group leader.

There is another instinct, and this is for the young of both sexes, and that is to play with each other. This is an important instinct as we are a group creature and this behaviour helps to form bonds and also helps physical development. This is a realistic outline for the human race. You see similar types of behaviour in other group creatures, but the main point is that we were like it prior to the change. Something had to come along, either a mutation of one of the instincts, or a biochemical or physical change. So what was it that happened to us that would allow for such change? Well, I thought long and hard on what it could be. All instincts had to start somewhere and it was an instinctive element which altered. It is very simple because it is something which we have now that we did not have then. The limiting factor to our intelligence progressing was that if we started to use objects as weapons within the group, we would have become far too violent.

The thing which came to start our evolution is quite simply LOVE: the ability of a male and female to fall in love with each other. You see, the way we were before love came along remains exactly the same as it always was, we still have all of the instincts that we had before. We still have the same number of the group that we had before, we still have a group leader, we still have a territory, and we still have the same eating and drinking requirements. We have to look closely at the group to see that the new instinct fits in and changes things. It would be very easy for this instinct to become part of the whole groups make up. I say this because we can live the new way and the old way even today. I call the old way the "fall back" way of life. It was never in our species' advantage it to disappear. The group now has much less aggression, with males much less likely to want to challenge for the leadership role, because we are now in a position for all males to assume the mantle of leader. We now have the birth of a family, where every male's instinct to lead is met, and every female's need to want to be with a leader is also met. I call the family a "mini unit", so we now have a group made up of smaller groups, and the way the genetic information is handed down has altered. Although the requirements of the group have not changed as a whole, we now have competition between the mini groups. Intelligence now can develop because the limiting factor of violence no longer applies, because the males all have the instinct to lead satisfied, and the instinct to mate is also satisfied. The cement that binds a pair together for life is love, and this extends to the love of the pair's offspring as well. Every leader of every mini group has the instinct to want to provide or supply the needs of his group, his mini group. Should things not be working out well for the group as a whole, then the leader of each mini group could take the decision to move territory and set up his own group in a new territory. The desire for groups to extend into new areas would have been great, and the freedom that allowed for greater intelligence would have been amazing. The fall back way of life never died out, it is part of our makeup. Sadly, it kicks in when love fails. It ensures that young are born even when this happens. Sadly, that thing that limited us, namely the use of intelligence in the creation of weapons, would have been exceeded very quickly, and the instinct for males to fight together as a unit be called upon far too regularly. Technology should only prove to be for our advantage in the new way we are, the way of love, in the fall back way of life, technology kills.

4

What we now have to do is look at us as a species, with the instincts as they were, and how they are now. The new instinct, which is love, should be working and making us a more peaceful species. We need to see how healthy we are in terms of the rules of nature that apply to us. I feel qualified to comment on my country and be critical where I need to be; however, you may find that criticism applies to your country; it is up to you to decide.

It appears that much is going wrong, that the family unit is breaking down, and this should be the backbone of our society. The breakdown of the family unit causes adverse behaviour in society and in your country. Remember that when love fails, we resort to the fall back way of life, and we certainly are failing. What would happen to a modern society if we were leaning towards the fall back way of life? What would happen is that young would be born, but women would raise the young on their own. Men would become aggressive, in particular young men. Young males would be looking to challenge figures of authority. Technology or weapons would be used in aggression, the driving force being that young men feel that it is what females want. Young men associate violence with sex; it is part of the way we were before love came along and made us much more peaceful. What should be happening is young men and women should be falling in love, having young and raising them as a pair, a unit, or family. With the breakdown of the family unit, there is a rise in violence between men, and a rise in single mothers. The problems are not just with young adults, they extend right throughout society. If you look at the divorce rate, you will see that is very high: approximately one in three marriages ends in divorce, and that only tells part of the story. Basically, this statistic says that the family unit is not functioning as it should, and that there is a level of friction across the board between men and women. You can't say that everything is bad, because some young men and women do fall in love, have children, and live happily as a family. What I am talking about is trends, or the direction that we are going. When I said that I had completed the jigsaw and that it was a map or blueprint of life, I did exactly that. I found out the rules of nature that apply to us as a species. In the UK, which is my country, we have far too many influences steering us towards the fall back way of life.

Think about how women are seen or portrayed in our society; you see images of beautiful, sexy women and girls everywhere you look. In terms of advertising, it seems that sex sells product. In newspapers, magazines, on the television, on advertising hoardings, buses, on the underground, anywhere. Half-naked or in sexy underwear or sexy clothes, the image of a woman seems tied to sex, and you were brought up with these images from when you were born. You may think that there is nothing wrong with it being this way, it has been like it for a while now, and people are still going about their daily business, children are still being born. Well, if you think of religion as worshiping a god, then think of it as spending a lot of time and thought thinking about a very worthwhile subject. However, at what point does admiring and thinking about women as objects of sex become almost like a religion? How much time do you have to devote to it, before it is considered a religion? It is an interesting point and well worth time considering. Something else to consider is that being stimulated by women as objects of desire is fall back way of life thinking. Before love came along, the way we used to be, seeing the leader of the group mating with females would have been a stimulus for us to want to be in that role. In other words, witnessing the actual act of reproduction is a turn on, and so would make males want to challenge for leader position.

Something has happened over the last few decades which has put us back towards the fall back way of life. It is quite simple, and by applying the rules of nature relevant to us as a species, we can see where we are going wrong. Women are competing against themselves for the attention of men, they all want to stand out and attract the attention of a top male. If you look at the fashion industry and the way that girls dress, you can see that they all want to feel sexy or attractive to men. The instinct inside females to attract the attention of a leader male was always there and is still there, even in the way of love or the new way. Women get an instinctive reward for standing out above all other women, there is a whole industry attached to this instinct and that is the fashion and cosmetics industry.

You don't have to go back far in history to see when women dressed with a degree of responsibility. I have heard elderly women say that young girls these days are way too sexy and that they dress inappropriately. There was a degree of responsibility in days gone by, when women knew how to turn men on but chose not to.

There is an instinct inside all men to want to have sex with any female that makes herself available; it is just that in modern society, all girls are dressing in a sexy way and give the impression that they are available. Sadly, today, most young people have had multiple partners, and casual sex has almost become the norm, it is almost like it is a pastime. If you look at the fall back way of life, all females get to mate with a top male by making themselves available, but it is not all males that get to mate. There is one thing that will be happening and that you can't stop, and that is that people will fall in love, it will happen to everyone. The thing is in the fall back way of life, the relationship will be tested to the limit, because there is temptation for both male and female. Love, or the new way, should be strong enough to withstand the temptations of the flesh, but sadly too often, it is not. There is a relationship that should occur when a couple are in love, this is that the male should assume the role of leader or decision maker. If this happens, then the woman will be instinctively rewarded, because it is in her make up to be with a leader. The man will be doing what his instincts are telling him to do, and that is to lead, and that includes providing food or essentials. So, you see that not only are the couple in love with each other, but there is a special relationship that goes with it. Both parties in a love relationship are instinctively rewarded, not only are they in love, but sexually they will want to make love with each other. When young come along, this adds to the relationship. The woman will be instinctively rewarded by having young, as will the man, but the man has a mini unit or family of his own, and the woman has her own leader. In the way of love, everyone is a winner. Children will have a mother and father, who can show by example how a loving relationship should be. This is really important, a child needs to be shown the relationship between its mother and father. Sadly, in today's society, there is a negative example, which shows how not to do it. It appears that women over the last few decades have felt that they were treated unfairly. There is a feeling now that it is politically correct for women and men to be treated equally. In terms of the workplace, in terms of society, in terms of the relationship between men and women, whichever way you look at it there is a modern ideology changing the way we should be, into the way that we are now. If you look around the world, the relationship between men and women is different from country to country, and the role of the man in terms of dominance varies. Another variable is the way women are portrayed: are there images of women everywhere you look? How do they behave on television? Start to analyse your country, your society, your world, because the behaviour of your whole country will depend on the behaviour of women. So key is the relationship between women and men, that I can't stress it enough, and you must start looking at any relationship that you are in, and see if it can be improved upon. I want women to look at themselves as peacemakers, because women can bring out the best in a man, simply by the way that they handle them. Rest assured that the way of love will work its magic, all people in the world will fall in love at some point in their lives, but it is knowing how to look after it, that is the real trick.

If you look at the history of the world, you will see that war has been far too common. It is the instinct that can be part of a man's makeup, but it should be left alone and never called upon. If all men in a society were in love and had their own families to look after, the call to arms would be much less likely to happen. The overall mood of each country would be much less aggressive. Remember that men think of fighting as a way to be attractive to women in accordance with the fall back way of life. So you can think of man having double the desire to go to arms and engage in conflict. However, when these instincts were current to us, we were only going to bite our opponents and chase them off. Remember the rule, that without love, weapons would be used if we became any more intelligent. Well, weapons are getting more technical, and they are being used, from the simple knife on the streets to the laser-guided bomb on a government level.

We live very complicated lives these days and sometimes we need to stop and think for a while, that is what I want all people to do. Think about the human condition, think about family and friends, think about your community, bring happiness to people. We want people laughing and couples happily in love and without fighting each other.

5

With the invention of the silicon chip, we now have a jump forward in intelligence. What we have to do is analyse how this impacts us as a species. The obvious rule of nature that applies is that without love it would be a disadvantage, and would be used against mankind. Technology has created new weapons and is being used against man. This not only applies on this level but also impacts us all in day-to-day life.

The silicon chip can be very useful, or it can be used against us. What we really need are some rules or guidelines. We need to be protected from the ever-growing intelligence where it has a bad influence and concentrate on what good it can do. If you look at mobile phones, then this is largely a good invention, with the possible exception of bullying which may occur with the young. If you look at word processers, again, a very useful invention. I am writing this book on a laptop, and I consider this work to be for the benefit of all mankind. You see, it is what you do with it that is important.

Advances in the medical profession have been very good, and if I or any of my loved ones needed modern technology I would be more than happy to receive that treatment. It is, however, in business and commerce that we need to look more closely at technology and how it affects us as a species. If you think about technology as an ever-growing thing, and as machinery as becoming more and more clever and cheaper and cheaper, then you must conclude that human involvement must be displaced, even if it is by degrees.

In a modern factory, technology and the associated machinery is churning out masses of product ever cheaper and cheaper, and the human beings are at the end of production lines, packing, palletising, and transporting the product. What I don't like and want to see is human beings racing against technology and being treated ever more badly. In a battle between technology verses human beings, technology will always win, because it can work all day and night and does not need tea breaks or holidays or sick pay. Human beings are and have been for some while been competing and working up against machinery, and I think that human rights are becoming less and less important. You can begin to see that we need rules, like "without love technology would be used against us". You have to learn to think on different levels of thought for different things and question why things are the way they are. There are many things to think about. Take one thing at a time and apply the rules. If you look at gang culture, you will see groups of young adults occupying a territory, with a leader or leaders. Gangs will come into contact with other neighbouring gangs and there will be fighting. There will be weapons used in the form of knives and even guns. Of course, what should be happening is that these gang members should have been brought up in a loving, caring atmosphere, a community, a family, and they should be falling in love and turning their back on violence.

Instinctively, they are rewarded in different ways: one, they are a part of a group, two, they go into conflict as a group, three, the young men feel that if they hurt or kill that they will get the sexual attention of the females. They also occupy a known territory or area that they are familiar with. So, you can see that these gangs are living the ultimate fall back way of life, rewarded instinctively by each of the above. The opposite to this existence is rewarded differently but is much the preferred option, a loving family in an area they call home with young of their own, and their own family. To get this, the cycle has to be broken. You need to be brought up in a loving environment within a community and be shown by example how to do it. Antisocial behaviour should be discouraged from an early age. Therefore, being a responsible parent is essential. Come on, dads, get your mini units in order! There are many elements of human behaviour that influence the way people turn out. I hope to cover all of them in turn.

The way girls are brought up is absolutely critical to a society functioning well, and if this is not done successfully then weapons will be used. It is up to the females of our species to call the shots in regard to what they want from men. Women are the peacemakers of the world and the way they conduct themselves determines the way that men behave. Over the last few decades, the way that women conduct themselves has changed. There has been a female revolution of sorts, call it the women's liberation movement. Women have been brought up with the view that they have been treated unfairly by men in the past and so are demanding that they be treated as equals to men in every respect. It is very unhealthy for a society for one half of the population to be turned against the other half, which is in essence what has been happening with the population. You see, the adopted philosophy of women in the workplace and in society is carried over to life at home, and although love has existed in all of us, it has proved not to be sustainable in today's society. Something is happening which is tearing at the threads of the family unit. You can see with our rate of divorce that there is a level of conflict that is damaging to the family unit. I suggest that sexual politics is part of the problem, but it is not solely politicians that are to blame. Look at reform in normal education and also in religion. It seems that the message from every quarter is one of being anti-male, and women have learnt to treat men in the most appalling manner.

Violence and war are both tragic and a mistake. The instinct for man to act as a fighting unit with his fellow men comes from the fall back way of life. How can it be that a fault in a couple's relationship can make a country want to go to war? The answer is that politicians engage in conflict if the opinion polls show that this is the way the country wants to go. So, if marriage is not functioning as it should, then men will be influenced to be aggressive, as I have explained already. The whole mood of a country can be war-like. It may be that there is no real option, but it is the way that it works. If a country is not doing very well and maybe there is a shortage of food, then the population may be more easily called to be aggressive because of the fall back way of life. With the instinct to go into conflict, I don't think there is an IDS associated with not going into conflict.

One thing that I find quite disturbing is computer games. There are far too many killing games, and I think that these games are getting more and more graphic. It is normal for people to say, "well I had this when I was a kid, and it didn't do me any harm". Well, the point is that some young people are more vulnerable and impressionable than others. If young adults come from a rundown area, and were brought up without love, then the influence of these games could be very destructive indeed. Not everyone comes from a well-adjusted background, and it may be that one of your children is hurt or even killed by someone who is not. As young adults with a vote, their viewpoint matters. Remember the opinion polls and going into conflict, if they have been brought up playing war games, they may be much more inclined to get into conflict situations because they lack the reality of true war. The point that I am trying to make is that we want to avoid anything that influences us to be in any way violent. Remember one of your loved ones may be the victim of a violent crime of such a person, and there will be no point saying, "why were they allowed to play violent computer games?" because the damage will already be done.

Sport is an interesting thing to look at because you can see how important instincts are, and how they operate in terms of reward. It is mainly men that have an interest in sport, and the viewing figures should back this up. If we look at football, for example, then the obvious instinct to look at is the instinct of going into conflict as a unit or team. By supporting a team, once or twice a week you go into conflict with an opposing team, and if you win then you get instinctively rewarded. If your team loses, then you feel very bad, but you don't have long to wait for your next game and encounter. There is another instinctive reward associated with supporting a team and that is that you feel that you are in a group, you are a member of a group, and this extends to women as well as men. The instinct to support a team is stronger in men than it is in women, and there are a lot more men that support a football team. In terms of the football teams themselves, the players get the same instinctive rewards as the supporters but feel it even stronger, as they are actually doing the fighting so to speak. Sadly, for too much time in the past, the fans of opposing football teams have had clashes and there has been actual fighting, a very bad thing to happen. Two countries can go into battle with each other, and nobody gets hurt. So, you can see that sport is a good thing, and although I have spoken about football, the same logic can be applied to any other team sport. In terms of individual sports, the driving instinct of one-on-one battles is to be the winner or group leader, the same for women and men, but it will be stronger in men.

Films and television also need to be looked at. Both of these things are powerful influences on human behaviour. When you go to the cinema and watch a good film, then you experience different emotions and they can make you feel great. However, they can also make you feel violent. Also, they often glamorise war, violence, sex, greed, infidelity, anti-social behaviour, or love, charity, or any good emotion. The point I am trying to make is that there are too many films that bring out the bad in the human race, and too few that bring out the good. The whole mood of a country can be altered or influenced to the fall back way of life, and this can affect a country, a continent, or even the mood of the whole world. Normalising or glamorising war and violence or sex and infidelity is definitely a bad thing to do, and we should be more responsible with this form of media. However, the same applies to the newspapers, radio, or any media. The vast majority of influence is generally taking us towards the fall back way of life. If you don't think that all forms of media effect a society then you must think again because they have massive effect. For example, looking at soap operas, I have heard on many occasions people say that they had to stop watching a certain soap because they found it to be too depressing. The storylines that are created just to compete between themselves normalise all the bad things that happen in life, and we see these things night after night. Think about children and how they are influenced. We are changing the behaviour of our entire society because of the things we let them watch, or that which they see in normal everyday life.

The mini unit or family should be the strength and backbone of the country. It should be functioning, and it should be solid. However, it is not, and so something needs to be done about it. The family should have at the head of it a male leader, a dominant male. Decision-making should be down to the head of the household. That does not mean that the woman is ignored, but conflict between the woman and man should be discouraged wherever possible, and definitely not in front of children. Children should learn from an early age that this relationship is the way that a mother and father interact. Remember that all men are born to lead a group and will be instinctively rewarded by this role. Children should be raised to be polite, well-mannered, kind, and respectful of their elders. Basically, do your best and remember that we are group creatures and that we are in a society.

It is man's instinct to provide the essentials of life, namely food, water, heat and a roof over their heads, and it is the woman's instinct to want to be provided for, to want the best for her family, and to want to follow her very own leader. Unfortunately, success these days is measured in the amount of material possessions that a family has, when what's really important is how happy and content the family is. There are so many countries in the world where the population is very poor indeed, but where the children, the mother, and the father are all very happy, living a good, contented life. This shows that you don't need all of the wealth and material possessions that we in the West have got used to. I am not saying that there is anything wrong with owning wealth and objects, but what I am saying is that it should not figure as strongly as it does, and that a family's happiness is more important.

What is happening is that men have, by association, linked wealth and appearing to be wealthy with being an alpha male and being seen to be a good leader. So, a man, if he looks prosperous, feels that he will be attracting women, and this is by and large the case. If a man has a big, expensive car, he feels that he will be pulling the girls in, the same with all material possessions. For women, they see the same link, and so are attracted to wealthy men and the easy life that goes with it. For less well-off communities, the young men have to be seen to be the alpha male, and they do this by fighting. They feel that if they fight and win, that they will get the girls.

It is a woman's instinct to want to stand out above other women and to look the best she possibly can. There are two very large industries associated with this, one is the fashion industry and the other is the cosmetics industry. If we look at the fashion industry, we can see that in one way women want to dress in the latest fashion, so they all look similar, but in the same token, they want to stand out as individuals. They want to stand out to attract a leader male, and this manifests itself by women dressing in a sexy manner. Fashion designers have learnt how to design sexy clothes, to make a woman an object of desire and lust. Women are trying to be seen as beautiful and sexy as they can to feel instinctively rewarded. However, there must be much thought about how it influences a society, both on a family scale and on the wider scale. There is fashion for men as well, but you can see that is much less important than it is for women. If you look in any big clothes store, you can see that the men's section is significantly smaller than the women's section. Really, we are playing an instinct game, with all the rewards and the opposite IDS links that go with not doing very well. If you look around the world, you can see that in some countries women can dress as sexy as they like, and in other countries women are made to cover themselves completely. So what is right? I think that both of these things are wrong, and that a woman can dress smartly and be pretty without evoking lustful feelings in men.

Sexual politics are a minefield. Such are the complexities of our human makeup, in fact, all politics are a minefield. We as a species, for both men and women, have the instinct to follow a male leader, and you can see that most countries have men at the head of their political ladders. This is not because men are nasty and horrible, it is just that we naturally want to follow the lead of a male. Leading a country is just like we were before we had love and started on our road of evolution. If a country is doing well and everyone has enough money for the essentials, like food, water, heat, etc., then the leader's position is not threatened. If, however, people are finding it hard to make ends meet, then it is natural to want to replace the leader, the same way we would have done it on a small group scale in the past. Politicians and leaders of countries can sometimes be there for the wrong reasons; they could hold office just to feel good about themselves and to get the instinctive rewards of being a leader. Some leaders want their countries to have a war-like footing, and so evoke war-like feelings in their population, just to feel good about themselves and to feel that they are attractive to the opposite sex. There is no fairer way of having a leader than having a democracy, by voting in your leader, but you must always look closely at their policies and question their motives for holding office. Further, if your country has not been run right for a period of time, then you will not be functioning or behaving as you should be. Your own knowledge or wisdom could be called into question, and you could end with things getting even worse. You could end up with an inappropriate leader; so make sure you know what you're doing when you vote.

The way that women are portrayed in society has profound implications on the behaviour and mood of your country. In some countries you see images of beautiful, sexy girls all over the place in the form of advertisements. Picture after picture of semi-clad women, or even naked women, all selling a product of some description. Sex sells product, and it is images of women that are generally used. You have to question what this does to people when they are confronted by such images. There is also the fact that children see these images, right from their earliest years. The power of images of sexy women has become the driving force of economies in far too many places around the world. Also, at what point does the sexy image become the advert for itself? In other words, when does the woman become the product of desire? Men will look at the adverts and will want to have a woman just like the one in the picture. We can't all have perfect-looking partners, there are not enough to go around. Think also about women looking at these images. They will feel very down about themselves. Also, the association between the image of sex and the woman will be endorsed, by which I mean the power that a woman has over that of a man.

Pornography, in the form of magazines and videos, is an industry in its own right. You see, pictures of naked women and images of people having sex is very much a turn on. This comes from the way we were before love came along, which is now the fall back way of life. You see, something had to make younger males want to challenge for leader position and that thing was seeing a pair in the act of reproduction, and so the visual image of sex was the driving force to challenge for position, with sex being the instinctive reward. I don't have any more to add on this subject other than to say that is a bad influence in any relationship that you are in, and it makes you look at women as objects of sex, instead of looking at the finer points of women.

6

One of my rules, which is that it is a disadvantage to be any more intelligent than you need to be in order to survive as you are as a species, needs to be looked at more closely. Intelligence over and above that which a species needs to do its essential tasks is a disadvantage because the increase would affect behaviour, and the species would not be doing everything that it needs to do to survive.

With the human race, love suddenly turned up, which would make us more peaceful and allowed intelligence to grow without us destroying ourselves. With each passing generation, our knowledge would grow, we would pass on information, and slowly but surely our intelligence would be improved. Now, with the invention of the silicon chip and the birth of computers, we have a sudden massive jump forward in intelligence, but we still have love. Or do we? How are we living our lives? Is it the new way, with love? Or is it the old way, the fall back way of life? The divorce rate indicates that love is struggling, but we are always going to have love cropping up. However, we are living much too much in the fall back way of life, for reasons that I have written about earlier.

When thinking about love or the fall back way of life, you have to apply it to different scales of thought: yourself, your family, your community, your society, your country, your continent, and the whole world.

The rules do apply to all scales of thought, and if we could get the whole world to live the way of love, instead of the fall back way of life then we will have cracked it, peace on earth.

It seems complicated, but really it is not. These things are achievable, and I think that if you could convince seventy percent of the population, then the other thirty percent would follow in time. Seventy percent would be my target and anything over that would be a bonus, although I live in hope.

We have lots of hurdles to cross in the courses of our lifetimes, on an individual level and on a world level. One thing that we have to do on a world level is to combat global warming. If we could all focus on this problem and all pull together, then technology would become our friend. This is the route that we should be taking. We have technology to make machines that can churn out millions of the same product, for very little money, so why not solar cells? Build the machines and make them by the billion, every single roof on every single house could be covered in them. The cost of the new solar panelling would be recovered by the saving in your normal electricity costs. I should say that with today's technology, if you were generating too much for your needs, you could sell electricity back to your normal supplier. The cells could be incorporated in your normal concrete roof tiles, with a wire running along the tile batten, and you just clip the cells onto the wire as you are laying the roof. All new houses could have this easily, and all old houses could have it for virtually the same price. The funding of the operation could be found with great ease, because it is a safe investment. All people have to pay for their electricity, so why not pay a financier? When your roof is paid for, even if it takes five, ten, fifteen years, you would get free electricity from then on. Obviously, I have not looked into this, but it is a very real possibility, and without a doubt it would work. This is technology and silicon chips doing what they should be doing: saving us from destroying ourselves, and not helping to destroy ourselves.

With the rule of nature that intelligence would be used against us if we were living the fall back way of life, we have to look at the world today. Not everything is at the extreme, by which I mean we are not either in love or killing each other with weapons. But the mood of the whole country and how people interact with each other could also be altered. In other words, behaviour or how nice people are with each other, this could be affected. The fall back way of life helps to create more demand for products, as I have already explained and for the reasons that I have said. If couples are splitting up, then both parties have to have somewhere to live, so we have demand for more housing. All in all, the fall back way of life, and all its influences is good for an economy, but bad for families and communities.

Silicon chips work well in large factories, and they make a lot of product. The product has to be made, transported, and sold. As we are now a global economy, one has to say that products are likely to transported a very long way. The factories require a great deal of energy to manufacture the actual product, the product is then packaged, and it takes energy to make the packaging. The product is then transported to its final destination. It has to be handled various times on its route. Cranes and forklift trucks, lorries and ships, all have to be made to cope with the increased volume of cheap product. It takes energy to manufacture all of these pieces of machinery, which handle and transport, and it takes energy to operate all the pieces of machinery to transport the goods. The energy comes in large by burning fossil fuels, by burning gas and coal to generate the necessary electricity and burning oil-based products to move the transporting vehicles around. Governments like their countries to export goods because it brings money into their economies, and governments will keep their economies in a financial condition that favours the exporting of products.

You see, silicon chips are everywhere, and as time goes by their influence will become stronger and stronger, even if you have to look really hard for them. What we must do is to concentrate on looking after human beings, to concentrate on the good things that men and women can do with their hands. To me, a piece of handmade furniture is a work of art. I admire the skills of artisans. If we all had one original painting hanging in our houses, that would generate so many jobs. If we all had one piece of handmade furniture, so many more jobs. We could all go to the theatre and see shows and plays, we could all go to restaurants and pubs, we could all do with supporting the human race. Machines are already encroaching into our lives; in the future it will be a lot more. Machines will get better and better and more complicated, so we absolutely must have some code of ethics or rules to protect ourselves. A moral code of conduct is what is needed, so that instead of shareholders boasting about how few people it employs, it will boast about how many people it employs. This is a big thing that is happening to the human race and we really do need to protect for now, but more importantly for the future. We have to look after the planet, and the human race, and all creatures, great and small. I do see the odd wind turbine and the occasional roof with solar panels, which makes me feel good, but we need a lot more. Also, electric cars, we want to see plenty of them.

If we could focus the world on seriously combating global warming and looking after love and loved ones, then that is the right route to be on. Remember the rule: intelligence only becomes a disadvantage when love and the family unit is not working. If you give love a chance, the old way will be forgotten when your mini unit is up and running as it should be. The violence and dangers will become history; that is a very good destination. I speak of forgiveness, your own and that of others. If you look at the influences that are in all of our lives, there are reasons why certain behaviours exists. We have to decide the direction that we take it is part of the human makeup, and is a decision that we all must take, the final destination is peace on earth.

If your country's economy collapses, you must resist the temptation to go and kill other people. It is a mistake within us, it is part of the fall back way of life, and never forget it. If it happens, then rise to the new challenges together and stand united. Be peaceful and calm and make decisions together as a family, your own family and the family of the world. You will not starve, the sun will shine, and plants will grow, the rain will come. Family, food, water, and sunshine, that is all that we need.

So why is this book called *Dancing Bears*? Well, if you look at dancing bears, you will see that when they are not performing they are suffering from mental stress, they rock their heads from side to side, clearly in distress. So, they dance to the tune of a higher intelligence, but they are not doing exactly what bears should be doing and so suffer from mental health problems. I draw a comparison to the human race, who is also dancing to the tune of a higher intelligence, and who is also suffering from mental health problems for exactly the same reasons.

When I first wrote *Dancing Bears* it rolled off my brother's printer on the 26th of June, 1998. I came home all excited. After a while, I turned on the television and the news was on. The first story which was being covered was that dancing bears were being banned in Turkey, and I mean the very second the television went on was the beginning of the coverage of the story. After a while, I thought, "good for you, dancing bears", and it was proof that as an act of decision from a human being, that a creature could be set free to live the way nature intended. Good luck, dancing bears, I hope you enjoy your lives, at least now you are dancing to the right tune. Dancing bears, you give me hope, we all need to be dancing to the right tune.

Part Two

1

I was about to find out that I was kind of hallmarked for hell, although I never believed in either heaven or hell. I guess I was to make the most detailed account of human behaviour possible, and that includes looking at religion and how it affects us. I was beginning to feel that I was a bit important because *Dancing Bears* was a little bit religious in the way it turned out, and I have a number associated with me that is mentioned in the Bible. That number is 666. You see, my date of birth is 6-6-63. I was to find out that the three parts of the date of birth was important because it doubles the importance of the numbers that it is with. So, you see, I have the ultimate date of birth for being a person. That should be looked at closely, because it is in the Bible. As I have said earlier, I did not believe in the afterlife or God or the devil, but I was to find out that all of these things exist. Also, I was to find out that the devil did not like me and that he had crossed my path at various points in my life, all of which I never knew. There had to be reasons why I would be targeted. These reasons I would find out by going to church and listening to all that was said in the church. It transpires that Jesus is meant to be coming again, something that I never knew. Also, I found out that all churches face east in the United Kingdom because they look to the east for the second coming of Christ. I was born on the east coast. Further, there has to be a Bryan present to witness the second coming of

Christ. Well, my older brother is named Bryan. So these are the reasons why I should attract the attention of the devil: I have the 666 number, I was born in the east, and I have a brother called Bryan. That narrows it down a bit as to why I was targeted, but the one thing that propelled me to the top of the leaderboard was writing *Dancing Bears*, because when he comes he shall bring a new wisdom with him.

It all started with my two dogs, Suzy and Poppy. I was in a really angry mood one night because something had happened to both of them. The fur on their faces was standing on end, and they would not look at me. They were behaving very oddly indeed, totally out of character. The speech that I came out with, I really don't know where it came from, the words just came. I said, "you are pure evil, you are the devil". I then went on to say that *Dancing Bears* would be published, and that love would thrive and grow. That the whole world would be in love, and that I come with the number 666, and that would make people believe it. Well, the dogs' faces went back to normal and they went back to their normal selves. Just as suddenly as it came, they went back to normal. Over the next few days, the dogs were sometimes their usual selves and sometimes they were totally alien creatures. On the news there was coverage of troubles in Israel. It was described as a storm of hate that engulfed the region. Well, I wanted to find out more about it, so I went and bought a newspaper. I opened it up and laid it on the living room floor, with a two-page spread covering the terrible violence and death. I was so interested in reading the coverage that I left it on the floor for two or three days. There was something in the feature for me to find. I had a feeling inside me that kept drawing me back to it, and then I suddenly knew what it was. In the feature there was reference to dates of when it all kicked off. I back-tracked through the last week or so and found out that all the violence started the day after I gave the devil speech, the day the dogs first went strange.

I could not believe it, but it was true. I kept back-tracking through the days of the week, and it absolutely was the truth. I laid down the law to the devil, and the very next day a storm of hate hits the Holy Land. I was beginning to think that I was a little bit special and important, and the magnitude of what could have happened was mind-blowing. Meanwhile, the dogs were half normal and half abnormal. There was definitely something wrong with them, but I did not know what it was. I found that buying the particular paper that I chose very fortuitous, and buying a newspaper was to prove very important one more time. I can't remember how far apart the two newspaper incidences were, it may have been days apart, or a week or two. The main thing is that I had a real urge that I had to buy another paper. I felt compelled to buy one. I went to the shop, which was just around the corner. I looked at all the papers and could not decide which one to buy. Eventually, I just chose one at random, and I still did not know what I was looking for. But then, when I got to the door of the shop, I spotted it. There was a small picture of

Satan at the top of the paper. It momentarily took my breath away. I could not seem to get away from the devil. The picture of the devil was advertising a feature story in the paper. I was to read the feature, and then was to do something absolutely remarkable.

The feature covered an interview with a Catholic priest who was an exorcist, and was talking about doing exorcisms, and what sorts of things happened. It said that exorcisms are always done in Latin and that they always start by saying *"Ecce Crucium Domini"*. It also said that there can be upwards of thirty spirits inside someone. Also, that when a sprit is exorcized, the person that it is happening to may retch, and their eyes may twitch. I thought about the article for a number of hours, and started to think about the spirits of the dead and my dogs. I thought to myself, "what if the spirits can go into dogs as well as people?" There was only one thing for it, I was going to have to try and do an exorcism myself, on both of my dogs. You see, this would account for the change in their personalities. Sometimes they were my dogs, and sometimes they could hardly look at me. The change in their behaviour switched several times a day, and I used to estimate how long in the day that they were normal. It could be 80/20, or 50/50, or whatever, but if it was the spirits, then they were definitely coming and going, and I knew now that this is what was happening.

There was one problem, and that was that I was never taught Latin, but I did remember that there was Latin on my life-saving medallion. I tried to remember it and the best I could come up with was this: *qum cuncu miseram videris hominum scias*. This means, "whomsoever you see in distress, you shall endeavour to assist", or something similar to that. Well, that was all that I had so I had to go with, and it was quite an appropriate translation I thought.

The scene was set. I waited a short while, until the time was right. Suzy was sitting on the floor, and Poppy was standing next to her. I got their attention and then I said it: *"Ecce crucium domini qum cuncu miseram videris hominum scias"*. What happened was totally unbelievable. Poppy was clear, there were no spirits in her, but Suzy was not. She had a kind of fit, her eyes and her face and muzzle were all twitching violently. And then, after about five seconds, she stopped twitching and she retched as if she was going to be sick. But that was not the end of it, shortly after this, Poppy spotted something across the room. She growled and ran across the room and snapped her teeth together; she was biting nothing but air. There was something in the room that I could not see but Poppy could. In actual fact, it was the spirit of a dead person.

I was obviously completely shocked and taken aback, frightened, scared, you name it, I was it. What I witnessed, I had never seen a dog do that before, and dogs don't understand Latin, so it had to be that I had done an exorcism. I had seen Poppy run across the room and snap her teeth together two or three months earlier, in my bedroom, so that meant that I had had this problem for some time. The realisation of my predicament was really frightening, and the implications on my life were massive. I had just learnt that there was an afterlife. But not only that, it was after me. I thought to myself, "How long has this been going on?" When I was a child I had a dog and I saw him growling and snapping his teeth at something in the room that I could not see. For three days I was really frightened, all sorts of things were going through my mind, not least that the trouble in the Holy Land was looking more and more likely that it was down to me. Then there is the devil, and the number 666, that living people were directing the spirits, that devil worshippers were after me. What about my family and my loved ones, are they in danger? All these things were going through my mind, and all in an atmosphere of fear. I was also concerned for my life, because people and the spirits wanted me dead, and they had tried to kill me in the past. Even though the dogs had become almost like my enemy, I kept them near to me all the time. When I thought they had a spirit in them, I tried to get rid of them using the same line of Latin as before, but it was not to work again. I think that when I first did it, I caught them off-guard and they were not expecting it, but afterwards they knew what was coming, and braced themselves for it. I made myself a cross out of two carpenter's pencils bound together with insulating tape. The dogs did not like it and would not look at it, but it was not enough to scare the spirits away. One of my first instincts was to get a Catholic priest, to get them to chase the spirits away. I found out where a local priest was and posted a letter through his door. About a week or two later he phoned me. I went to see him one evening and told him what had been happening. He listened with great interest, but did not give me any help, except to give me the telephone number of Northamptonshire's exorcist. I met the exorcist one evening, and I again explained my story and asked him if he could come and get the spirits to leave and not come back. He said that even if the spirits were in a person, he would have get instruction from the highest levels, and said that he could not do it to dogs. It was looking as though I was on my own with this problem, and I was not going to get help from the Church. At the end of the third day of being frightened, I ran a bath. Before I got in it, I dipped my finger in and made the sign of the cross on my forehead. All of a sudden, all the fear I had just vanished. I was back to my normal self. You see, I had reasoned that the spirits and the devil worshippers had not managed to kill me in all the years that they had been trying, so I felt reasonably safe with this thought in my mind. I had spent a lot of the past three days going back over my life to try and look for the devil worshippers and the spirits of the dead and how they got to me.

What I decided to do was to fight the devil, fight the spirits, fight the devil worshippers any way I could. I was not going to go down without a fight. I had to take stock of the situation. What information did I have to hand at that point in time? I wrote a list of all the facts I could think of relating to the devil and the spirits of the dead. For example, they can go into living creatures, such as human beings or dogs, and that they can move very fast. That they can influence the behaviour and thoughts of the person or animal that they are in. That someone can have multiple spirits put on them, or even that they can walk through walls. I can't remember all the facts that I listed, but it was quite a lot, and just like the above. Now that I was aware of what was happening, I kept on my guard for spirits entering my body, and I kept an eye on my dogs. When I thought that there was a spirit in one or both of the dogs I would try and get rid of them. If you like, I was trying to do an exorcism on them. I initially had good success by saying prayers. The spirits were frightened by the Lord's Prayer, or my favourite prayer, the Holy Michael Prayer for protection. At this point in time, I was working and had a long drive every morning and every evening, with both of the dogs on the back seat. What was happening was that the dogs were being loaded up with spirit when we were at home, and they were releasing the spirits onto me while I was driving. The objective of this exercise was to make me have an accident, preferably fatal. But now I knew what was going on, I could do something about it. At that time, it was to recite a prayer. Early on I had good results with praying, but there came a time when the spirits just would not go, they would just sit it out. It became a battle for me trying to get my dogs back to normal, but the spirits just would not leave them be. I could not ignore the fact that living devil worshippers were organising and directing the spirits on to me via the dogs. You see, my enemy was a network of people loyal to the devil, who did not want me around anymore. They feared that someone with the number

666 was going to turn up, and wanted to expose them and destroy them.

If you are quiet and still, and preferably in the dark so that you have the minimum distractions, you can feel a spirit enter your body. There are two main types, one from the spirit world direct, and these feel like a shadow moving into you. The other type comes from being inside a devil worshipper, direct from person to person, and these spirits are highly charged, like static electricity entering your body.

In the newspaper article about the devil and exorcisms, it said whenever spirits inside someone were asked what their name was, they always replied by saying that they were the devil or Satan. After the three days of fear, on the fourth day I did something quite remarkable. I had been thinking all day about the spirits trapped in hell, and hell being here on earth. I was wondering how it could be that they did not go to heaven. Because I had spent so much time thinking about forgiveness, I thought how could be that they were denied entrance to heaven. And then it occurred to me that maybe they had the spirits of the dead inside them when they died, and that these spirits could maybe grab hold of their spirit when it left their body. On the evening of the fourth day, I decided that I would put it to the test. I had the dogs and the spirits in my cottage, so I could communicate with the spirit world. I was sure that there was a spirit or spirits inside Poppy, and so I said, "If I was to ask you what your name is, you would answer by saying that you were the devil, but you are not the devil, you are just a spirit of a dead person". Well, the reaction I got was quite remarkable. Poppy started jumping around the room. She was so excited she just could not stop leaping about the room. In all my years of having dogs I had never seen anything like it, a dog that can understand every word that you say. I was on a roll and I wanted to capitalise on my situation, so I said, "Yours is the kingdom of heaven, you are to go to heaven this very night, come into my dogs and then go heaven". Suzy and Poppy were both laying down now and they went to sleep, and I could continue with the spirits. When I said come into the dogs, both Suzy and Poppy were fitting, jerking, and twitching. Then when I said, "Go to the kingdom of heaven", the twitching would stop, and the dogs would lay still. So I would say it again, "Come into the dogs", and the fitting would start again. This went on until the early hours of the morning, until I thought that the dogs had had enough. Every time I said, "come into the dogs", the spirits in the room did just that. I knew this because this was something I could actually see, fitting dogs. I don't know if these spirits actually did make it to heaven that night, but I strongly think that they did because of the feeling inside me. You see, I felt a feeling of love and happiness every time I said, "go to heaven" and I felt that I was doing the right thing.

I learnt a few things that night. I learnt that the spirits did not want to be in hell, that they wanted to go to heaven. I learnt that when they enter another living creature, they can hear and see just like they were alive. I learnt also that I was very important as a person and that the spirits believed in me, and I think that what I did that night was what I was meant to do.

2

The spirits kept on coming, and were occupying Suzy and Poppy, and I was spending more and more time trying to get the spirits out them. One night, both of the dogs started to do something weird. Their eyes turned completely scarlet, their inner eyelids were coming over their eyes, and it was very scary to see. Neither of the dogs had ever done it before, and they both started doing it at the same time. I had to get a video recorder to keep a record of the events that were happening in the cottage. I borrowed one and started filming the dogs. I wanted proof of the dogs' eyes. It was hard to get a good shot of the dogs because the battery in the recorder only lasted a short while, and so I had to guess when to start filming, but I did manage to get some good shots. I remember one night I said that line of Latin to Suzy and Poppy, and Suzy got up and came right up to me. She was barking and growling and snapping her teeth together. I stopped her biting me by grabbing hold of her collar and held her away from me until she calmed down and backed off. I had had Suzy for a number of years, and she never was aggressive in any way, shape, or form, but she was after I said some Latin. So what does that mean? Well, it means that she had the spirit of a dead person inside her, and that the spirit was telling that her that he was going to be forced out. You see, I was learning all the time. I learnt that a spirit could occupy a dog or a human being and that the behaviour could be affected. They could make you aggressive and violent. The spirits that were coming into the dogs were getting increasingly violent and nasty. They were becoming less scared of prayers and Latin, and they were getting ever bolder. You must remember that I was still working and travelling to work with the dogs on the back seat.

The spirits of the dead were in death as they were in life. There is as much variation in personalities as there is in living people now. The spirits of the dead are just as fast in terms of thinking as we are in life. They are not some fuzzy little apparition, they are as complete a person as you are in life, except they are in spirit form.

I was to have another good night's work with the dogs. I got some holy water from the local church, and I wanted to conduct an experiment with the dogs. The dogs were downstairs in the living room, and I was upstairs in my bedroom. I had set up the video recorder to aim it onto myself. I explained what I was going to do, and that was to put holy water on the dogs and video them to record what happened. Before I used the holy water, I would sprinkle normal tap water on them just to show that if there was a reaction with the holy water that it was not just that the dogs were scared of water, which they were not. Both of the dogs were laying down and were awake, so I flicked some tap water on the dogs from a glass. They licked it but they were not really interested. Then I went to change the glass to that of the holy water. I sprinkled it on Suzy first, and again, there was no reaction. Then it was Poppy's turn. Poppy almost immediately got up and ran across the room. I told her to go to bed, which she did, and she sat there with her back arched and all the hair on her head and hair down her back stood on end. She was in that position for a few minutes. So this time, Poppy had a spirit in her. I said that the holy water is not the killer of all killers, but they sure don't like it, and I got all of it on video. I could think of three reasons why the dogs were having the spirits put on them. Firstly, so that the devil worshippers would know what I was up to; secondly, so that I could be attacked whenever and wherever I was; thirdly, so that they could turn the dogs against me and make me isolated and alone so that I would be miserable. I was to go to the church regularly, and was learning about my church and religion every time that I went. I was also learning about fighting the devil. Anything to do with the scum Satan made me even more interested because I was turning out to be quite some devil fighter. I was a little dismayed at the way the church let me down, and left me all alone. I did say one night to my local priest, "Well I suppose I will have to fight him on my own". The only positive thing that he did was give a glass of holy water. My life was stuck in a rut. I had the dogs constantly being attacked, and me being attacked via the dogs.

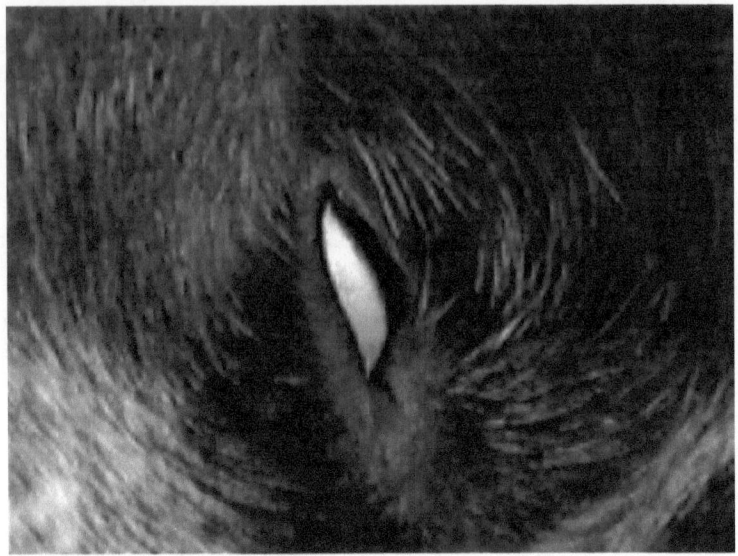

The eyes of both of the dogs went like this every time the spirits entered them. This image was taken directly after the application of the holy water.

This image was taken directly after the application of the holy water. Poppy adopted a strange, hunched up pose and all the hair on her body was standing on end, which you can see.

This image shows both dogs at the same time. This is important to note that Suzy and Poppy both had exactly the same problems with the spirits.

This image is very similar but it was taken at least half an hour after the previous image was taken.

There came a point in time when I had to make a terrible decision, and that was to have the dogs put to sleep at the vets. I had been thinking that it was the only way for some time, but obviously it was a very hard decision to follow through. It was the morning of taking the dogs to the vets, and I thought that I would like to take some footage of them running about, something to remember them by. So I took them to the local park and took a last video. I was so choked up, but they were a danger to me and other people; there was no other way. Before I had them put to sleep, one day when I knew that there was a bad spirit in Poppy, I said to the spirit, "try to talk". You see, I had been trying to befriend it. Poppy lowered her head and made a deep moaning sound. The spirit was trying to speak but he could not manage it, it was very sad.

The day I had the dogs put to sleep, I went to London with the video tapes. I wanted to go to the newspapers and show them what I had got. I managed to get inside the reception area of one of the larger papers. There was a telephone that you had to pick up. I explained about the dog tapes, but naturally they were not interested. I knew that there was no way I would be given the time to explain to anyone that I have evidence of the existence of the devil, it is video tapes of my dogs. Meanwhile, I went back to get to the cottage thinking that without the dogs I was going to be left in piece. Well, I had a very rude awakening. Life for me was to get one hundred times worse. The spirits started attacking me directly. It was no longer the occasional spirit from the dogs, it was spirit after spirit.

Praying and the holy water just was not good enough. There did not seem to be anything that I could do to defend myself. I thought, "there must be something I can do", I just did not know what it was. I went and laid down on my bed and I prayed to God and told him my situation. Almost straight away, I had the answer. The words of a song came into my head: "love is an energy". All I had to do was to learn how to turn love on to use it as a weapon. I concentrated on Jesus and Mary. I pictured images of them in my mind, and then it happened. From the back of my eyes, a bundle of love energy dropped down through my body. I could feel it because I had the spirits of the dead in me, and they were hurt by it. This was the start of me fighting back. I could actually hurt them. I did it once, so I could do it again, and each time I did it, it became easier. I could do it without thinking about Jesus and Mary. I spent the rest of my day lying on my bed fighting the spirits. The spirits were coming into me through my feet and up my legs and into my body, and I just kept driving them back down. I was so pleased that I was able to fight back, and I was to get stronger and stronger. It was like finding a muscle that you had never used before, so it was weak to start with, but got more powerful the more I used it. So love is an energy that hurts the spirits. In actual fact, love is hell's fire. And so, the spirits, when they are inside you, don't want you to feel love because it hurts them. So there is no nice way for a spirit to live in you, they have to destroy any feelings of love that you might have.

My enemy was not just the spirit world, but also living people who worship the devil. These people have spirits of the dead inside them. They use them in any way they can. They can direct the spirits onto other people to get across whatever message they want. They can make other people want to have sex with them. This is mainly what they do, they use them to get sex. But they can put other messages inside you. For example, they could make you feel suicidal. Devil worshipers worship sex and they go to orgies and say words about the devil. The spirits take part in these orgies as well. I knew that my life was in danger from the spirits and from living people, who could stab me or shoot me, or hit me over the head with something heavy. It was not very nice not knowing who your enemy was, it could have been anyone walking down the street. I just had to get on with my life the best I could and try and ignore the dangers whilst being sensible. The spirits had learnt how to attack me with my new defences. They learnt that if several spirits attacked me at the same time, they could overwhelm my defences. I had to explore my mind for new ways to defend myself, along the same lines of that which I had already learnt. I came up with many different ways of delivering love energy, and each time I came up with something new I would get the upper hand for a while. But then the spirits would learn how to overcome the defence and change their attack. You see, the spirits were learning about me at the same time that I was learning about them, it was a running battle. Every day I would get better and better, and what I wanted to do was to attack the spirits outside of my body so that I could start attacking them while they were in other people. I believe that I did achieve this, but because it was outside my body, I could not feel it so I can't say for definite. I had taken to going to my local pub so that the devil worshippers could get near to me and attack me with the spirits, and so I could practice attacking outside of my body, and see by the reaction on the faces of the people that the spirits were in, if I was successful or not. That is why I think I did achieve it. I wanted to fight the devil any way I could, so I thought about the internet. I thought, "How can I get a website created?". I spoke to my friend, and he gave me the telephone number of someone who creates websites. And so that was it, all I had to do was work out what I wanted to say. I spent five days thinking how I could destroy the devil worshippers. What I came up with was something like this:

> "Satan, you satanic scum, I promised you that I will dig you hole so deep it will take you a thousand years to rear your ugly head. This is for all devil worshipping scum, all those people deal with spirits of the dead. You back off and leave me and my loved ones alone. You are to cease immediately your devil worshiping ways, and you are going to write a full and detailed account of all of your time as a devil worshipper, every little thing that you have done wrong is to be written in a confession. The whole spirit of this exercise is to destroy your empire, and so every name and address of anyone you know to be a devil worshipper is to be recorded. You have six

days to write your account. At the end of this time, you are to take one copy to the police and one copy to a Roman Catholic priest. At the end of this time you are to receive a mark on the forehead, and that mark may as well be the number that was to be my curse, 666. If you have been a devil worshiper for less than three years, then you don't have to take the mark, but still have to make your confession as above. Anyone with the mark is never to be seen with anyone else with the mark, you are to stay apart. The spirits of the dead that you use do not want to be in hell, they want to go heaven. When I offered them forgiveness, they did not have to think for a second, they just took it straight away. That is how I know that when you die you will not want to be in hell. So what I am offering is a once only deal: forgiveness of all sins and a place in heaven. You will also be free to be in love again without being punished by the spirits. Of course, the people who confess and take the mark will have to be very religious for the rest of their lives, because if there are spirits left on earth they will target the people with the mark because they turned against Satan. Everyone that comes across a person with the mark should treat them with respect and kindness because what they did in taking the mark took great bravery."

I have not got a copy of the actual website, but that above was very close to it. On the website was a copy of *Dancing Bears*. It was important that *Dancing Bears* was part of the website, because I offered it forward as a work of wisdom.

3

So, I had a website, but I was told that it could take several weeks for it to be picked up on the system. So, there was a quiet period. The devil worshippers had calmed down, and there was a lull in the fighting a period, a kind of rest. Unfortunately, a new chapter of my life was about to start. I had told my family all about what was happening, and they went to my doctor. He contacted the mental health team, and they took an interest in me. I thought that with the video tapes, they might believe me. So, I told them the story of what had been happening, but they refused to look at the tapes, and suggested that I go into hospital for a few days' rest. I thought it would be good to rest away from the cottage, so I agreed. I thought that God wanted me to go, and I was right, because I was to learn something very important.

In the cottage, I felt that I had tamed the devil worshippers. I was only getting the occasional attack, and it was nothing I could not cope with. Now in hospital, I found a whole new branch of satanic activity. There were lots and lots of spirits, and they were hopping from patient to patient. They were mainly what I call "head shots", and this means they directly put their head into your head, like overlaying one central nervous system over another. They did not have a clue as to what I could do, it was like they had to learn everything from scratch. The devil worshippers that I had fought in the past were organised, but these spirits they were not. It was like a lot of spirits, but each one was doing their own thing, they were not acting as a team.

I think that a spirit is made of electricity or some form of electromagnetism made as an exact replication of the whole of your nervous system. Physics that we can only dream of has been combined with our biology to create the afterlife. What the spirits in the hospital were doing was, as I said, they were overlaying their spirit onto others' bodies. Some nerves will line up and they will experience life as a part-living human being, but it will vary according to the percentage of the match of the nervous systems. If the spirit has a good match, it will stay in you; if it is a bad match, it will go on to the next person. You are in death as you are in life, so there were a lot of spirits around that were mentally ill when they were alive. So the system repeats itself; if a spirit has a good percentage match, it will stay put, and then you have a mentally ill person. It is the same with normal people and normal spirits: if the spirit has a good match, it live your life to a degree, it can actually influence your thoughts. If you like, it can take you over a little bit, and live your life with you. The mentally ill spirits know that the Christian faith treats them as an enemy, and will drive them out where possible, although not nearly to the degree that I would like to see. What I really want is for all spirits to go to heaven, with the exception of one, Satan himself. There is no room in heaven for the devil, and in a thousand years' time, we will have the technology to deal with him ourselves.

Meanwhile, I still had a battle on my hands. I still had to deal with the new spiritual problem that I encountered in hospital. The number of spirits that were attacking me was growing all the time; it was almost as if the word had got out. I was using all the techniques that I had learnt from before, and with much success, but things were about to get worse. I believed that the devil worshippers had found out where I was because I was getting high energy spirits again, and in batches, typical satanic attacks. This was on top of mentally ill spirits. For three days and two nights I only got about one hour's sleep; I was exhausted. I decided to go back to the cottage for a rest. I got a taxi from the hospital to Northampton town centre, where I had a few beers and then got a taxi to the cottage. After a couple of days, the mental health team asked if I was coming back. I had had a rest, so I was ready for more fighting. It was nothing like it had been when I fought solidly for three days. It was much calmer, but nevertheless, I was still fighting the spirits, but it was manageable.

In the hospital there were copies of the New Testament, and I decided that I would read it. There were a few things relating to me, and one of the things was in Luke's gospel: when the second coming of Christ comes, he shall have a crown of gold. This was relevant to me because my hair was turning a gold colour. I think it was due to the drugs that they were giving me, but I am not sure. The streaks of golden hair were so vivid that they attracted the attention of the other patients. I was a little bit the centre of attention for a while, and it was another important thing that pointed towards me being the second coming of Christ. I got further into the Bible, and was very shocked when I reached Revelations 13:18, where it says that someone will turn up with the number 666, and will put the mark on either the right hand or on the forehead. When I wrote my website page, I knew that the people had to be marked to keep them apart for their rehabilitation, and also to identify them. I chose the forehead instead of the hand, but this was just another thing which points towards me being the second coming of Christ. Another thing which was amazing was that it says he shall thrust Satan into hell and seal him for a thousand years, well you know in my website, I said that I would dig you a hole so deep, that it would be a thousand years before you raise your ugly head. Yet again, more evidence that I was the person in the Bible that was meant to turn up. All these things that I said and wrote about that I read in the Bible were things for me, to make me believe that I was the second coming of Christ, even though I was too scared to admit it, because I knew that people would think I was mentally ill if I said it. I wanted the Church to look at me. As I said to Father Damien, I was labelled by God to be looked at, and that the devil read the label, and did not like what it said. The devil and the devil worshippers, and the spirit world, all wanted me dead, and to preferably end up in hell. Well, I was not to lay down and die, I was going to fight. I had myself and my loved ones to consider. The devil and the living, and the army of spirits, were all out for me. But I never gave them any reason to hope. I was to fight them every step of the way, and the devil worshipping scum were on the backfoot. I was a one-man army against them, and I would never lay down and die. It is said that when the second coming of Christ comes, that he will defeat an army alone with a cross, and that is what I intend to do. My cross, which on one occasion was drawn in anger in Muswell Hill in London, I still have. The battle started in the Seven Sisters area of London, where the devil had closed in on me. I felt as though the devil had got me cornered and that I had no place to run. I felt that the underground was a deathtrap, and that I had to stay above ground. So, after the initial danger, I took a few buses, and said to the conductor, "three stops please", or "two stops please". I thought that it would be hard for them to track me down. I was right: I was hard to track down, but track me down they did. They cornered me in a pub at the bottom of Muswell Hill. I thought I was safe, but I was wrong. If you could imagine it, there were loads of devil worshipping scum in the area, all looking for me and with the intention of killing me. I had little or no defence with me, I had to rely on my instincts and my faith to deliver me through this problem. My faith in God had grown to the very highest level over the last few weeks, and I knew that I was going to be a hard nut to crack, if they were going to get to me at all. I ended up walking a long way, but eventually felt safe enough to get a taxi from Barnet to Great Billing, and my cottage. I felt safe there because if they killed me there, then there would be a reason to kill me. If I was killed in London or miles away, it just could be a random killing, but if it was at my home then there could be a reason to kill me, a line for police enquiries. This is what my life had become, a constant battle. I was living on my wits, not knowing from one day to the next what was going to happen. It was very hard, but my new faith would see me through. I grew in strength with every passing day. I would go to mass several times a week, and each time my wisdom and faith would grow. The battle of Seven Sisters came the day after I had Suzy and Poppy put to sleep by the vet. The adrenalin was keeping me going, and I thought that I would go the distance for them and their memory. I loved my two dogs, and they were a part of my family. I had lost something very dear to me, but I had the devil to fight. A fight that I could not stop, and one that I never called for, a fight which made sense of my whole life. I have to say that I have taken to fighting the devil like a duck to water. It has come naturally to me, and we have to face facts, I have some biblical pedigree for the job. I have been thinking about myself. I am not without sin. In fact, I have been a big sinner. It is not something that I am proud of, but I am everything that I need to be to do the job. The job being the destruction of hell. Remember that hell only exists here on earth, and that the spirits of the dead should not be here, they should be in heaven. So, if you can rescue all of the spirits that are stuck in hell, then hell no longer exists. Therefore, everyone is destined for heaven. It sounds very simple, but the devil has grown strong over the last few thousand years, and every soul he takes to hell becomes a soul-taker for the future. The devil has to be taken out of the picture, and I have done this. On the 11th April,

2002 at 1.30 am, Satan entered my body. On the 9th and 10th of April, I had been directing the spirits of the dead from hell into heaven, stealing from Satan. Obviously Satan was not happy with this, and although I had given up all hope of the scum Satan coming to me in battle, eventually he had to come, because without the spirits, hell does not exist, and he would not have an empire. Having spent two days directing the spirits from hell into heaven, the scum Satan did not have a choice, he had to come to me, even though I had given up all hope of meeting him. The coward devil sought to enter my body from behind in a direct overlay. This means that he was full size and tried to slide his body into mine. Having spent the previous two days rescuing the spirits from hell, I was used to spirits entering and leaving my body. Satan was like no other spirit, he was between fifty and a hundred times stronger than a normal spirit. Well, Satan went down, and the last words he heard were, "we don't want any shit like that", and these were my words. Suddenly, he was hit from above, and I saw him with my mind disappearing backwards into the planet. He was going back, first his arms and legs flailing, and he was screaming, and then he disappeared. I did not have a very long look at him, but he was between five foot eight and five foot nine in height. I know this because I am just short of six foot in height, and he was some way short of filling my frame.

Although he was disappearing backwards into the planet, at some speed, I did get a little look at him. He looked a bit like Steve Mcqueen, that is as close as I can get to describing him. He was not fat, he was lean. He was athletic in build, a very powerful spirit indeed. I should imagine that if Satan ever got inside you that you would do anything that he wanted you to, no matter how bad. Better that the scum be out of the picture for a thousand years, and better, in a thousand years he be got rid of for good. By then we should know how to do it. Do not ever give in to Satan, for the rest of history of the human race. He will worm his way into the human race and promise you the world and will take everything. Always be on your guard. The devil is a human being who worked out how to have his own empire. He knew the rules but decided to bend them to his own ends. There never should have been a devil, but there is one. What we have to do is deny him a future. Satan is the scum of the earth, but he does have substantial clout when fighting the spirits. To his own ends, he cannot be ignored. The devil is a force to be reckoned with and cannot be ignored. I wish it was not true, but it is. The devil cannot leave us alone, and he has a hold over us. It is us up to us to alter the odds, we have to learn to fight. The stakes are very high, but the rewards are equally as high. Freedom from the spirit world is not to be taken lightly, it has to be earned. Satan has been around for a long time and has been our enemy for a long time. He has sought to undo us from the outset, the devil is pure evil. If he can do anything evil, then it will be done. When fighting the devil, there is one thing that you have to remember, and that is, if it is evil and it can be done, it will be done. You see, the devil cannot contain his evil, and he gives himself away every time. You must always remember this rule because it is very important. If you are analysing your family and are trying to track down the devil, you must always bear it in mind. You see, the devil can't contain his evil, and it gives him away every time. We have not got very much to go at, or so it seems. But with this rule you can track the bastard down. Never underestimate the depths to which Satan will go with his evil. The devil will even occupy a dog and turn it into a vicious killer, even on a baby. Satan is so evil that it makes it hard to sleep at night, but you must, you cannot let him win. Holy water will chase most spirits away, especially if you repeat over a number of days. There is also praying, you can pray and you can get your family to join in. Remember the importance of love, this is the ultimate weapon against evil. In an ideal world, we would all have been raised in an atmosphere of love, and we would know it, and then raise their children the same. Not only is love a nice feeling, but it is actually doing you good. You can't get enough of it, and don't forget there is IDS for love as well as your other instincts. This is feeling not very good and having a vacuum in your life. We need love to blossom and grow. To give love is as important as it is to receive it, because you are instinctively rewarded for giving and receiving love. I never used to believe in God, or have a faith, there was a vacuum inside me but I did not know it. I was beginning to believe that there was a God when I was writing *Dancing Bears*, but I refused to believe in the devil and hell. Ignorance of religion is a weakness, and the gap is better filled. I became a Roman Catholic when I first discovered that I was being attacked by the devil. It was an obvious choice for me because of the number 666, and holy water and fighting the devil, and promoting love, and above all there is a female icon of love and that is Mary. Whatever your religion, there will be love because it is so important. I hope that you believe in a negative force as well as a loving force, by which I am referring to the devil. I also hope that you believe in an afterlife, because there really is one. This is one of those things where it is either black or white, there is no grey area in between, there either is or there is not.

Satan has been behind so much war and bloodshed. I know this because of the trouble in the Holy Land: a storm of hate starting the day after I laid down the law to the devil. He was so angry that he could not contain his evil. He gave himself away. Satan and his army of spirits can easily stir up anger and hate by entering people and making people feel these emotions, and that is how they operate. They can pick on a small number of people and load them up with spirits and put the ideas of violence and hatred in them. These people then go and commit murder, so hostility between countries and religions is fuelled, and will escalate. Satan loves the fact that we have different religions, because he can play one off against another, and has been doing it for thousands of years. It is the same as playing off one country against another. In order for us to have world peace, it would make it a lot easier if the spirits were all gone to heaven, or have the second death in combat, either way they would be taken out of the equation. In my battle with Satan and his army, I must have given the second death to so many spirits, and injured and wounded many more. I really don't know how many it is. It was an easy choice for me to take, because they were trying to kill me, and also I don't think that the spirits here on earth are very happy. I looked as the second death as a release from hell. Some spirits have been so evil in their time on this planet that they could never imagine that they would be welcome in heaven. It needed someone like me to convince the spirits to go to heaven. They will believe me because I fought them, and they know in the world of the spirits, that I am the person with the three 666 that was due to turn up and defeat the devil. They will believe me, and that is what is necessary: belief! Living people may not believe me, it is the dead that are more important. I am here for them, and I am here for the living as well. If I can destroy hell by removing all of the spirits, then the living are protected from their input. I am going a long way in protecting the human race from the scum Satan, and I can do it! The potential enormity of what I am proposing is mind blowing, but it is something that I have to cope with.

The intelligence that is involved, God and me and the devil, I am just a cog in the machine, as is Satan and as is God. Because I am the man on the ground, so to speak, I have a large degree of responsibility to do that which is right. I think about God and the devil and myself and how I fit in. There is much to think about. It is like a battle of the minds. I think of something and the devil counters it, then the devil thinks of something and I counter that. It is a running moving battle, and really, God is running the whole show, we just cannot see it at times. God is so intelligent that we cannot predict his movements, we must go with our instincts, and go with God. Satan is so far out thought of, that it is hard to think of his next move. It is a good job that I only have to think every now and then. Satan's only purpose is to undermine that of the human race. He seeks to undo us at every turn and destroy us wherever possible. It is our duty to fight Satan wherever he rears his ugly head. Satan will have us dancing to his every tune. We must always dance to our own tune. Satan is to be pushed into the background. Satan is always to be fought. He is always to be questioned, the human race must outthink him. It must always be that Satan is fought to the bitter end, because he will always try to beat you. Satan is the scum of the universe, he is a human being but must be considered not one, because of the pain that he causes. There must always be a force to counter that which is evil, and it must always be a force for good. It is my belief that good will overcome evil, and that evil will be defeated. The human condition is one where the human race defeats that which is normal, and yet becomes the truth. To defeat that is by example, and to know this is by the truth.

If you are a child and your family shows you no love, then look towards God, and Jesus and Mary, and if you have brothers and sisters let them do the same, because you are always going to be loved, and you must spread the word. You will never be left alone, and when I say never I meant it. You must believe in me because I am from God, and what I tell you is the truth. I will always touch you God if you are with me.

4

I think that it is important to summarise the things that I have learnt, to take stock of the situation. To describe hell, the devil, and the spirit world here on earth. How does it all operate? Why do the spirits do what they do? That is, to undermine the human race and destroy love wherever possible. The word "devil" refers to the actual devil himself, but also all of the spirits that are here on earth, they are also all known collectively as the devil. I found out certain things about the spirits, such as, they move around really fast. I know this because when I laid down the law to the devil, the resulting storm of hate happened really quickly afterwards, and that was on the other side of the world. Also, the spirits can alter their size and shape. I know this because of the battles I had with them, and having them in my body, things which I could feel. Further, I saw my dog Poppy run across the room and snap her teeth at nothing but fresh air. She was attacking a spirit in the room. You see, dogs can sometimes see the spirits. On that occasion, she was looking at something not very tall, maybe two feet high. And so you can see that with relatively little information you can start to build a picture of what is really happening. My two dogs, Suzy and Poppy, were being used to attack me. They were also being used to keep an eye on me so that the devil worshippers would know what I was up to. There are two fundamental types of spirits. One is a spirit from the spirit world, and when these enter you, it feels like there is a shadow entering into your body. The other sort is a spirit coming from a devil worshipper, and these feel like static electricity entering your body. When being attacked by a devil worshipper, they come in groups of between twenty to thirty, and the amount of strength of the charge will vary from devil worshipper to devil worshipper. I remember on one occasion, I was being attacked by four different devil worshippers one after the other. I could tell this by the different strengths of the different groups of spirits. The spirits of the dead do not like not being inside a person, or maybe a dog or any other creature. It may be that they get cold or weak when they don't have a host to be inside. When the spirits are in a person they can affect the mood of that person; they can turn you on with their thoughts, or they can make you miserable or even suicidal, they could make you aggressive or violent. They can certainly make a dog very savage, and when I hear of a baby or toddler being attacked by a savage dog, I think of how evil the spirits can be. It is the knowledge of the spirits, of what they can do or behave in a certain way that makes me want to do something about it. Praying can be the first line of defence against an attack by the devil. Some spirits are easily frightened and may exit your body at the first line of a prayer. Holy water is another line of defence, it is not the killer of all killers but they sure don't like it. One thing to bear in mind is that spirits are human beings, and as such, their characters will vary from person to person. In life you meet all sorts of people, some can be nasty and aggressive, some less so, and some people can be very nice. Well, it is the same in the spirit world, but there is one thing that cannot be altered, and that is that there is no nice way for any spirit, good or bad, to occupy a host. I learnt that love is your protection. It is an energy, it is hell's fire, it is what hurts the spirits. And so, if a spirit is occupying your body, it must influence you away from love. In *Dancing Bears*, I talk of two ways to live your life. The first is the way of love, in which the love that you feel becomes your protection. The other way is the fall back way of life, and there is no protection from the spirits if you live your life this way, there will be no hell's fire to rescue you. This is why all spirits that remain on this planet are to be treated as your enemy, because there is no nice way for a spirit to occupy a host. It is my belief that it is the destiny of all human beings to go to heaven when they die, and that any spirit trapped on this planet is there because when they died they had a spirit or spirits inside them at the point of death.

When directing the spirits to heaven, I found that it was skyward, and so it is not on this planet, but in space. I put much thought into the subject of forgiveness when I was writing *Dancing Bears*, and I knew of the two ways to live your life. I knew of the influences that there are which can affect your behaviour, of the circumstances of fate that are dealt to you. We can all be good or, equally, we can all be bad.

Life for me at the hospital was getting better. The attacks were much less frequent and, eventually, I stumbled upon a way to get rid of any spirit that entered my body. I call it the total burn, a way of killing any spirit that was in my body. You think of love or hell's fire burning right through your body. I had done it, I had beaten the spirit world. The spirits knew that I was way too hot to handle and they completely stopped attacking me. I was happy to tell the doctors that the spirits had stopped, and they were very happy to let me go back to a normal life. I was to be going to my church, which was Roman Catholic. I was to be given lessons about the church and was to be baptised a Roman Catholic, and then more lessons, then I was to be confirmed. I could not forget what had happened to me, about my battles with the devil and the spirit world, it was to dominate my life. I knew that I had to re-write *Dancing Bears*, because when I wrote *Dancing Bears 2*, I was full of anger and there was no way it would ever get published. As a person, I had become more timid, there was not much fight left in me, and I could not see a way of defeating the spirit world. It is still out there, and the spirits are still going about their evil business. It is this book, *Dancing Bears 3*, that I hope will do the trick. If I get my way, then the devil worshippers will give up their wicked way of life and take the mark and become Christian, and all the spirits will use me to go to heaven. When you go to war, you get scared. My scares are to my mind, because, if you can imagine it, I have living human beings that worship the devil, and they do not want to be exposed and beaten. They have wanted me dead for countless years, and they used the spirits to try and kill me, but they have not yet succeeded.

Although they cannot easily get in me, the spirits could go for people that are around me, they could hurt me by hurting the ones I love. On the night of 30–31st March, 2011, my lovely fiancée, Karen, died. I was to wake up and find her dead. As yet, there is no indication of what she died of. It was a mysterious death, and me not knowing means I cannot rule out the devil. Since her death, my resolve to do the job has been growing by the month. You see, even if she died of natural causes, there are people falling fowl of the devil every day, and I believe that I can stop it.

5

I am going to write this chapter under the assumption that I am indeed the second coming of Christ. Of course, I may or may not be, but it is just that it makes sense that way. In order to make all the facts fit, you have to look at the whole picture, and then when everything fits into place, you know you have the truth.

I was born on the 6th of June 1963, which gives the date of birth 6-6-63. This is how it is normally written, so I have a number associated with me. Everyone has a number in their date of birth, and this only occurs one day in every one hundred years, and so it is very specific to each individual. I have already covered that, so I won't go into it again, but it is very important that is the point. I was not to know any of the facts about the second coming of Christ. In fact, I did not even know that he was to come again. So, an individual was born who, without knowledge, would be labelled sufficiently that the devil and his whole army of spirits would hunt him down. Their aim was to stop him being recognised or to stop him from fulfilling his destiny. If they could kill him, they would take his soul to hell. Obviously, I am talking about myself. I never knew any of the facts which I have previously highlighted, I was not even to believe in God or the devil, and only had a basic Christian education at school. It was vitally important that I be raised this way, because if I had been raised with a strong religious conviction then I would never have questioned how we came to be here. *Dancing Bears* would never have happened, and I hope you see the potential importance of the work. The devil, who was after my soul and my life, was not sure that I was the one, not until I came up with *Dancing Bears*, and that pretty well sealed my fate. I would like very much to know the fate of other males born on 6-6-63.

If the devil had left me alone and not gone after me, then none of this would have happened. It was only his input in my life that made me seek answers. The devil worshippers, who targeted me and put their spirits onto me, should have left me alone. They made me think that I was someone important and fuelled the fight. In all my young life, I never thought that my date of birth had any real significance, and just associated it with the anniversary of the D-day landings of the Second World War. I was never raised thinking that I was someone special, or anything to do with religion. I never thought about my date of birth as being anything special, not until I wrote *Dancing Bears*. Then I thought that it was important, or at least an amazing coincidence. Here I was coming up with a work of wisdom, almost a religious piece of work, and I have a religious number associated with me that is mentioned in the Bible. If you look at all of the things that point towards me being the second coming of Christ, or just amazing religious coincidences, then it makes very interesting reading.

We have already looked at the 666 and the implications of this, so we have a devil fighter that has the number of the three sixes associated with him. All of the churches in the UK face towards the East, because this is where they look for the coming of their saviour. Well, I was born in Scarborough, which is on the east coast.

When the second coming of Christ happens, there must be a Bryan present to witness it happening, well I have got an older brother called Bryan.

The second coming of Christ will bring with him great wisdom. Well, my wisdom is *Dancing Bears*. You must read this and give this the credibility you think it deserves. The second half of *Dancing Bears*, which is this book, also becomes part of the wisdom.

When he comes again, he will judge the living and the dead. Well, I did this, and this will also happen in the final battle, which is yet to come.

When he comes again, he will defeat an army alone with a cross and be seen by the whole world. Well, I have been fighting the devil alone, all the spirits and the living devil worshippers. What possible army could one man defeat alone other than that? I have defeated the army on a personal level, but it will only be complete and entire in the final battle if I am successful.

When he comes again, he will banish Satan for one thousand years. I did that on 11th April 2002; and what's more is that I said to the devil that I would dig him a hole so deep that it would take him a thousand years to rear his ugly head. I said that to the devil long before I found out that it was written down and was meant to happen.

In Revelations 13:18, it says that someone will come along and defeat Satan and will put a mark on either the right hand or on the forehead. When I wrote my website, I knew that the devil worshippers had to be marked, for two reasons. Firstly to keep them apart because it is necessary that they are not seen together, and secondly, so that normal people can identify who they are. I chose to put the mark on the forehead, but I did consider the right hand for quite a long period of time. The mark was to be the number, which was to be my curse: 666. I felt that I had the authority to do this, and when I created my website I had no knowledge that this was meant to happen.

It is written that when the son of man comes again he shall have a crown of gold. Well, when I was in hospital, I developed golden streaks in my hair. They may come back at some point. It was not just blonde, it was truly golden.

On two totally separate occasions, I have been asked by children specifically if I was Jesus. This had nothing to do with me having long hair, because at the time I had short hair. It is said that children shall know who the son of man is. I have also been told that I was Jesus by many adults, although nobody knows exactly what he looks like, people think that I look like him.

In the Bible, in Revelations 13:18, it refers to the number 666 as the name of a person and says, "let him who can calculate the number or understand the number be the one whose name it stands for". Although this is not saying that this person is the son of man, there is no doubt that I am the person with that name, the person mentioned in Revelations. The only thing that is important is that you make the link between the second coming of Christ with that specific part of the Bible, and the number or name of 666. If you make the link, then the whole picture becomes complete. It is a reason that would make the devil look for me, and thus instigate the battle between us. There is only one battle where one man can defeat an army alone, and that is this one, the army of the spirits and the army of the living who are servants of the devil.

The calculation referred to is a statistical analysis of me, that says I can only be the second coming of Christ. If you were to guess the odds against all of the above points, you would find the odds for me being the son of man would be colossal, in favour of me being the person we have been waiting for.

I approached the church to give me some help but was to get none. I really was all alone in my fight against the devil. As it transpires, this was the exact thing that should have happened, because I had to work out the truth without prejudices or other people's incorrect input. It is my belief that hell is here on earth, and that it only exists because the spirits are trapped here. If they could be rescued and given the chance to go to heaven, then hell will no longer exist. I have put so much time into thinking about forgiveness, thinking about rehabilitation and reasons why people have gone wrong and have done bad things. The influences on human beings are very great and very real, all as explained in Part One of *Dancing Bears*. We need to know how to achieve the very best that we can in life, as individuals and as members of society and families. Satan and all the spirits trapped in hell, like the fall back way of life, they don't get burnt if you live your lives this way, because love does not kick in and harm them. So, you could say that the devil is for the fall back way of life, and the way of love is for the way of God. So you can see that *Dancing Bears* is linked to religion, and this becomes the work of wisdom that is meant to come about, the work of wisdom that the son of man will bring when he comes again. And so you see, there really is no other option, I have to be him.

The job that I have to do is to destroy hell. How do I know this? How do I know what my job is? It comes down to forgiveness, because my philosophy calls for great forgiveness of sin, and the fact is everyone is destined to go to heaven, everyone except Satan. Who is going to forgive the dead? Who is going to get all the dead to heaven? There has to be someone to come along and do something about it, someone that will be believed by the spirits. That person is me, because I fought the spirit world, and I know that they think I am that person.

When I first wrote *Dancing Bears*, when I found out how we came to evolve and what rules of nature apply to us, everything just fitted into place. Everything became clear, and then I knew the truth. It is like that with this half of the book, the same thought processes, the same methodical application of logic, and the same truth.

I was to learn about my new knowledge and religion, and I am very happy to call myself a Roman Catholic. I was baptised and confirmed. I do, however, have an open mind about other religions and know that we share a lot of common ground. It is this common ground that different religions should concentrate their energies on, what we share, not what is different. I refer back to the day that when I laid down the law to the devil, and the rapid response of the devil: the storm of hate that hit the Holy Land. Satan is playing one religion against another. He is using our differences against ourselves. Therefore, we should do the exact opposite to what he wants. This is how you fight the devil, united not divided. I have learnt to look at other people with different religions and nationalities as cousins. If you accept my work, then we are all related to each other, we all share the same love, love that started us on our journey to being human beings. Imagine how good it would be if all peoples of the world accepted where we came from, that we started from a single point in time and space.

I believe that the very first love came from God, that God was waiting for the exact right species to evolve in nature, to add the magic ingredient, and start us on the journey, which brings us to where we are now. Unfortunately, "now" is not in very good health at the moment, there are far too many things going wrong in the world.

There is reason for us to be optimistic for the future, and this optimism comes from my observations of the human race as it is at the moment. I look at my own country and look at how we are too strongly drawn to the fall back way of life. If I was to criticise my own country, I feel that I have the right to do this. However, if you feel that the same things apply to your country, then you can make wise decisions about what route you want to take.

Wisdom is a very powerful word, and I want people around the world to concentrate on becoming wiser and apply this wisdom to their own lives and the lives of their loved ones, and of their societies or communities. We all strive to be happy. "Happy" is a key word, our objective is to all be happy, but we don't just want it for ourselves, we want it for everyone that we know and love. Love is the key to happiness, and we must know the rules of nature that applies to it, to look after it and nurture it. Love is a sacrament from God. So when you are happy and in love, you should be thinking of God and thanking him. When you are sad and miserable, these are negative feelings. Remember that this is how the devil wants you to feel, and you certainly don't thank him for that. So we have positive and negative forces acting upon us. It is very easy to determine which one is acting upon you by how you feel, and you can act accordingly.

It is my desire to destroy Satan and his empire and do away with hell. If I were to be successful, what would be the state of play? What would be happening then? The human race would change completely, because the negative element in terms of the devil would no longer exist. But you still would have the fall back way of life to contend with. All of the influences on our behaviour would still be there, as per *Dancing Bears* Part One. I want all people to believe that there is an afterlife, and to know that we will live forever. The time we have as living flesh and blood should be a good time, and so we have a duty to live life a certain way and use that time in accordance with the way of love and the way of God. Even if you choose to not believe in God and an afterlife, you should still live life in accordance with *Dancing Bears* Part One. To get the very best from life, you should observe the rules of nature as I have laid them out to be and remember your instincts.

What you have to do is remember that there are two ways to live your life, the way of love, and the fallback way of life, the way of God or the way of the devil. One way will bring you happiness, and the other will bring you pain and misery, it is down to choice. God is real, he does exist, and he will help you when you need help. He will help you in different ways, no matter how subtle it is, he will help you.

Dancing Bears is written in two parts, but both halves are part of the same story, they are linked. The wisdom, which is what this book is, tells you how to live your life and get the best from it. So I ask you to look at your loved ones, your family and friends, and start to apply the wisdom. Look closely at your own behaviour, see if you are doing things wrong, and look at the influences that are acting upon you. It may seem that the task is too big, and too hard to tackle, but it is not. Look at your childhood and look at the influences that you had acting upon you. One thing that is very important is whether or not you were shown how to love. Were you raised by loving parents, in a happy stable environment? Far too many children are not getting these things, and so as a consequence, people are turning out flawed and damaged. If you are a parent, you must, by example, show your children how to interact and how two people can be happy; in other words, you must show love. Arguments and discord and tension and friction are far too common these days, and it is a terrible example to raise children in such an environment. *Dancing Bears* Part One shows you how to get the best from life, and you don't have to believe in God if you don't want to. But the way to live your life is coincidently the same; if you believe in God or not, the path or direction is the same for both ways.

I would like to add one further point on the subject of the religious path, and that is that if you don't have any actual love in your normal life, that you can get your love through God, and so there is always a safeguard against the devil and the fall back way of life. If you do not believe in God, you are missing out on love. Remember that you can't get too much love, it is an additional defence mechanism against the devil and the fall back way of life. I consider it to be a great strength to believe in God, it is not a weakness it is a strength. This philosophy that I call for, the unification of the human race, is absolute and fundamentally has to be done. The wisdom or the philosophy has to be applied to life, and you can do it.

Dancing Bears is a philosophy of life. I have learnt to live with the philosophy and to cope with the philosophy of life. I can tell you that my philosophy of life is true and is complete. What you need to do is to apply the wisdom to your own life, to give yourself leadership and direction. Life is not easy, sometimes it is hard, but what you sometimes have to do is rise to the occasion. Sometimes, logic dictates one direction, but wisdom another. You have to acquire the direction of your knowledge, of your direction of thought.

The work of wisdom that *Dancing Bears* is, has to apply to the whole of our human behaviour, and has to be compatible with everything that we are. There must be no errors, and the philosophy has to be complete, there is no room for error.

There has to be a point in time when you conclude that you have reached your destination, a point in time where you have to conclude that you reached a logic that cannot be improved upon. The blueprint of life that *Dancing Bears* is, is solid and complete. I have studied human behaviour in close detail, and hope that it you may find it as enlightening as I did, and as accurate. Don't forget that you are a human being with feelings, you can analyse yourself and how you feel in different situations, how your mood is affected by outside stimulus, by what is going on around you. Every human being is valuable. It does not matter what religion you are, the same laws of nature apply to us all, we all came from a central point. I find a good way to look it is to assume that we are all related, that we are all kind of cousins. When you meet a cousin that you have not seen for a long time, you say, "Hey cousin, how are you doing? What have been up to? Are you married? How many children have you got?" All manner of questions could be asked, but the main point is that through the way we act towards each other, this becomes an endorsement of our own values, of our own religions, of the good points of our lives.

Forgiveness is a big word, it is one the most important words in any language. We all must learn that if you feel that you yourself are forgiven, and how good that feels, that you extend that right to other people and other nations. Human behaviour has may influences. I want all people to look at themselves and learn to forgive themselves and others. If you have no faith, it does not matter, the forgiveness is for all people, because the rules of nature apply to all of us the same.

Love is another important word. There are different forms of love. The love you have for your friends and family, the love you have for your children, the love you have for your partner, the very intense love that bonds a couple together and is at the heart of the family unit. In *Dancing Bears* I explain that love came along and was the key ingredient for the beginning of the evolution of the human race.

I learnt that love was an energy and is in fact hell's fire. I learnt to use it as a weapon to defend myself. I fought the spirit world all alone and have been on this incredible journey of discovery, and I share it with you in this book. So where does love come from? I think that God introduced it to us, and I would like to explain an interesting line of philosophy to you. We think of ourselves as extremely intelligent now at this point in time, but just imagine what we will be like in a thousand years time, or a million years time. What physics and biology will be like. I think that we will be capable of biochemical alterations, to engineer an afterlife and also introduce love. Because we don't yet know that much information, we shy away from it, but really what will happen in the future?

I think that the human race has existed at least once before, on a different planet but very similar to our own. That the first time we existed we did not have an afterlife or spirit, but we did have love just the same as we have now. There was no devil or evil spirits to attack us or bring us down, and that we went the distance. We did not destroy ourselves in a nuclear war, but we found peace and happiness, and that we engineered an afterlife for ourselves, and also heaven as a place for us to go to. That on this planet now, God did some biochemical engineering, and created us, as we are now. I don't know where God came from. Maybe he was the perfect spirit of a human being from the first time we were here, I really don't know.

Unfortunately, the scum Satan decided to have his own empire, because he knew that he could do it, he had the wisdom. I like to think that Satan's work can be undone if I could get the spirits to accept forgiveness and go to heaven through me, because I have done it before but just not on that scale. This would be a wonderful thing to happen. Imagine a world with very few or even no spirits in, no negative force acting on individuals, that would be quite something. Satan has to be dealt with, by which I refer to the spirit world, as I have already dealt with the actual devil. He will not rear his ugly head for another thousand years. But, collectively, the spirits are also known as the devil and have to be dealt with.

I have had much to learn. I have endured much hardship and I carry scars of battle. The scars are mental, of the mind. People who knew me before and after my personal battle with the devil have said that I am much more timid than I was before. It has taken many years of living with what happened to me, and who I turned out to be, for me to rewrite *Dancing Bears*. Coming to terms with the enormous task and responsibility of what I have to do, for it comes down to just one man, and that is me. Can I go through the final battle which is yet to come? Can I be triumphant over evil and destroy hell and the devil? I don't know, but I believe that I should be given the chance, because the stakes are very, very high. You have to decide, and it is very much a personal decision, on the direction in which you want your life to take. Will it be the way of love and of God, or will it be the fall back way of life and of the devil? Only you can decide, and so you have to judge yourself, and decide what you are and what you want to be. Think also of your children or loved ones, because your decision will affect other people as well as yourself. Think about your community, your society, your country, and your world. What sort of world do you want to live in?

I believe that sometimes God gives certain people a job to do in life, and if you are given a job to do then you are compelled to do it. With me, I was given a job to do, but I was not told of it, I had no idea what was expected of me. I had to find out that I was labelled by God to be looked at. I had to find out that the devil had looked at me, and that he did not like what he saw. With *Dancing Bears*, this book, I became number one enemy of the devil. Something inside me made me question life, and when I found out the truth of how we came to be here, I wanted to do something about it. My philosophy could not be contained by one man, and because it was so valuable, it had to be shared, which is what *Dancing Bears* is all about. Love and the way of love is the enemy of the devil. The devil will punish any champion of love that he comes across. Although Satan was after my life and my soul, he was to come up against the philosophy of my book. Without knowing it, I was becoming a cause for good, a source of hatred by the devil. In a way, I was already victorious over the devil, because as an act of my own philosophy, I had changed the rules in my own life, and that was before I knew of God and the devil. When I found out what was happening to me and to all the people in the world, what pain the devil causes people, I chose to fight. This book is key in the fight against evil. It becomes the wisdom, the truth, and if I share the wisdom with everyone else, then the devil becomes unstuck. The tangle of lies and mess of evil becomes untangled, and the truth is seen, and with the wisdom comes a new freedom. A freedom to begin to fashion your own life, to make quality, informed decisions that affect yourself and others, including your loved ones and friends. God will always be there for you, and God has been with us all, fighting the devil by our side. No matter how strong the devil became, he never gave up his faith in love, and the good way to live our lives, the right route to be following. Love is stronger than evil, but that does not mean that evil is without strength and influence because it has both of these things. All people must become wise to the devil and wise to the truth to ensure that we make it, that we go the distance, that we do not destroy ourselves, and that we create heaven on earth.

I am nearing the end of *Dancing Bears*, but I hope that is the beginning of a new brighter future for all of us. There is the final battle for me on my own, a battle with the spirit world, and the destruction of the devil's empire, of which I hope to be successful. Learn to do things that you know God would like, and do not do things that you know the devil would like, it is as simple as that. Ask yourself this question, whose tune are you dancing to? The way of God and the way of love, or the way of the devil and the fall back way of life? You decide. It's your future; let's unite and make it a good one!

*Available worldwide from Amazon
and all good bookstores*

www.mtp.agency

mtp.agency

@mtp_agency

www.ingramcontent.com/pod-product-compliance
Lightning Source LLC
LaVergne TN
LVHW091602060526
838200LV00036B/965